T0295628

# Global Business in the Age of Destruction and Distraction

# Global Business in the Age of Destruction and Distraction

Mahesh Joshi
Gaurav Rastogi
J.R. Klein

OXFORD
UNIVERSITY PRESS

OXFORD
UNIVERSITY PRESS

Great Clarendon Street, Oxford, OX2 6DP,
United Kingdom

Oxford University Press is a department of the University of Oxford.
It furthers the University's objective of excellence in research, scholarship,
and education by publishing worldwide. Oxford is a registered trade mark of
Oxford University Press in the UK and in certain other countries



Impression: 1



Published in the United States of America by Oxford University Press
198 Madison Avenue, New York, NY 10016, United States of America

British Library Cataloguing in Publication Data
Data available

Library of Congress Control Number: 2022930111

ISBN 978–0–19–284713–3

DOI: 10.1093/oso/9780192847133.001.0001

Printed and bound by
CPI Group (UK) Ltd, Croydon, CR0 4YY

# Foreword

As the title of the book suggests, we are living and leading in the age of increasing destruction and distraction. In every sphere of life, politics, economics, or education, understanding common knowledge and the standards taught by education and experience have lost a bit of validity. Distraction mediated by technology has signalled the destruction of the old model of business and the nature of knowledge. Centuries of the old industrial education system creating uniform actors, actions, and behaviours once considered the gold standard no longer hold the same validity. The exponential rise and increase in ever-changing technology leads primarily to recalibrating the relationship between humans, technology, and culture. Add to that the stress, tension, and anxiety of a global pandemic and international aggression and the result is frustration and disparity in every corner of the globe. This raises the question, moving forward will we continue to be on this trajectory of destruction and distraction, or will we find a way to make these technologies our servants rather than masters?

The authors of this third book in their Global Business series deals with this destruction and distraction in a straightforward, rational, and practical manner. They not only examine the issues of systemic change and seemingly overwhelming challenges but also basic tools that have pragmatic applications for leaders, businesses, and individuals to address and transcend these challenges.

J.R. Klein, Mahesh Joshi, and Gaurav Rastogi have come to this book with extensive knowledge, experience, and understanding of not only the challenges but also the solutions available. Their tone and style are down to earth and provides an excellent set of tools for remaining relevant in the constantly changing world. As their first two books talked about globalization and the challenges of business, cultural, and social transformation, this instalment presents a remarkable pragmatic and valid approach to overwhelming issues by presenting strategies that will change thinking and behaviour.

Global Business in the Age of Destruction and Distraction is a must-read for leaders and anyone witnessing the volatile nature of change or is interested in staying relevant by thoughtful application of time-honoured solutions. It is a 'must read' for anyone who wants to be a positive transformational leader in the 21st century.

Dr Andrew White
Senior Fellow in Management Practice
Said Business School
University of Oxford

# Preface

The constancy of life has the tendency to be consuming. Please understand that being a consumer of life is a strategy embraced by many, myself included. However, being a consumer of it and having life consume you are two different concepts. I confess that while I subscribe to one, I am the victim of the other. Life's consumptive appetite is for time. It steals minutes, then hours, then vast periods of time that seem to vanish without a trace. Today this has moved beyond the pale of lack of attention to a weaponised system of distraction. Information and hypernarratives come at us from all directions. Distraction is ever-present.

Not long ago, my wife and I attended the All School Reunion of the high school from which we graduated. We visited with people with connections that went back to childhood, which seemed closer than the history it represented. Great memories of fun and friendliness seem fresh, but life, in its chariot of time, is hidden by memory which compresses the distance between two points. What seems fresh is placed by history 50 years in the past. The chariot can move quickly and blurs the scenery unless we stay alert. Moments of memory seem to be outside of time and give a different viewpoint of where we have been and where we are going.

It is from this perspective that my friends and I have written this book. The mistress of time is cloaked in an age of destruction and distraction. For some, it is a struggle to keep their eyes open, and history becomes a reality, with change becoming the destroyer of worlds. However, the chariot of memory seems to fold time, allowing us to use the past to choose the future. Just as those friends from years past look much different than my memories of them, they remain who they were. The relationship becomes the message. The benefits of successes and failures enable us to reinvent and revitalise who we are. This interconnection allows us to consume life and not worry about being consumed by it. When you lift your head above the blur of the journey, you can see all the mountain tops.

J.R. Klein

# Acknowledgement

Global business has become the centre of the upheavals caused by any of the issues on the planet. Geopolitics, nationalism, inequality, global warming, pandemic are all impacted by the basic fabric of global business. Some use it for the development of their countries and citizens. Some used it for political gains or to cover their ineffectiveness of governance and not the wellbeing of people. Others use it to build relationships and as a tool to counter the power or empowerment of others. Global business's driver, technology still played its role in providing connectivity.

J.R. and I welcome our new co-author Gaurav Rastogi for the third book in the Global Business series. He brings a holistic dimension for enhanced value to the content of this book. It was an amazing experience for us to connect very effectively and efficiently with the technologies from three separate locations to build the content for the book.

J.R. and I feel privileged to have a solid and supportive relationship with our classmates and faculty at Oxford University. The constant interactions on various platforms have enriched our knowledge and stoked our intellectual stimulation. We thank Oxford's classmates, alumni, and faculty for consistently feeding our growth as authors. We are also grateful to have the guidance from faculty, Andrew White, Marc Bertoneche, Lalit Johri and Sue Dobson. Thank you to Oxford University Press's Adam Swallow has guided us to develop and deliver quality content since the inception of the Global Business series. We acknowledge and thank those who have contributed content, constructive criticism and knowledge to this project, especially the team at VoiceAmerica.com led by Sandra Rogers, who has partnered to produce our radio show, Global Business with Mahesh Joshi on Voiceamerica.com. I also thank all the classmates and Alumni at Harvard Business School and London School of Economics and Political Science for their encouragement and enriching discussions which have always been a learning experience.

I feel indebted to my esteemed classmate at Oxford & co-author JR Klein and his wife, Lola. They have been longtime friends and a source of inspiration for a disciplined life and balance of social commitments and continuous intellectual development alongside spiritual underpinning in developing ideas and supporting the community. J.R. and I have had several long and intriguing discussions on diverse topics connected with Global Business.

My global experience with American multinational companies has been enhanced by working with Larsen & Toubro MAN Energy solutions (A Volkswagen Company). Professional business leaders such as Mr S. N. Subrahmanyan, Mr R. Shankar Raman, and Mr Subramanian Sarma at Larsen Toubro have provided a deep and rich experience that has taught me what it means to be an effective leader.

Recent opportunity has enabled working with MAN Energy Solutions (A Volkswagen group company). Its CEO Uwe Lauber, CFO Mr Jurgen Klopffer, Head of Human Relations Mr Martin Rosik, and CSO Mr Wayne Jones have provided an example of the passion for developing innovative modern technologies and the drive to relate to customers. The privilege to work and observe these leaders has helped in continuous learning and improvement.

I must thank the executives at various companies around the globe that have provided a plethora of learning experiences. These groups include ARAMCO, ADNOC, KOC, KNPC, PDO, SABIC, Reliance, Samsung, Hyundai, JGC, Mitsubishi, Chiyoda, Toyo, Technip, Bechtel, Flour, DOW, TATA, Tecnicas Reunidas, Tecnimont, Chevron, Exxon, BP, Shell, BPCL, EIL, QRC, Warren, Sunbelt, Schlumberger, GE, Linde, and ABB. Special thanks to the teams at ITER **and** CERN, the organizations researching nuclear fusion.

I acknowledge and thank our third co-author, Gaurav Rastogi, who rightly recognizes the support of his family Nidhi, Kush, and Adyah, along with his mentor Kailash Joshi, for encouragement and perspective. Gaurav also recognizes Rukmini Seshadri for her research and thinking, friends Rahul Sharma and Yogesh Virmani for their interest and conversations and Amit Garg and Sriram Padmanabhan for their wit and wisdom.

Finally, we acknowledge the great debt owed to the generations of thinkers and communicators that have been the foundation for wisdom in our time.

# Contents

# PART 1
# DESTRUCTION AND DISTRACTION

# 1
# Forced Into the Future

In 2019 society was faced with the unprecedented COVID-19 pandemic. Many countries and all 50 US states responded to the threat, in part, by issuing stay-at-home orders in spring 2020, most of which were lifted as transmission of the virus slowed. However, as parts of the world face a second and third wave of the spread of the virus, some stay-at-home orders have reappeared (Lee, 2021). The pandemic has had a significant impact on public health and everyday life, and especially on employment and the nature of where and how work gets done, accelerating the onset of a disruptive future for work. World Economic Forum Chair Klaus Schwab described the exponential change and related disruption anticipated from the combined forces of advances in automation, artificial intelligence, and technology as so pervasive, they amounted to the Fourth Industrial Revolution (Schwab, 2016). The level of disruption anticipated to be brought about by the Fourth Industrial Revolution, expected initially to span years if not decades, was collapsed, in some cases, into months or even days.

When pandemics sweep through societies, they upend critical structures, such as health systems and medical treatments, economic life, socioeconomic class structures and race relations, fundamental institutional arrangements, communities, and everyday family life. A Pew Research Center survey reports that 'A plurality of experts think sweeping societal change will make life worse for most people as greater inequality, rising authoritarianism and rampant misinformation take hold in the wake of the COVID-19 outbreak. Still, a portion believes life will be better in a "tele-everything" world where workplaces, health care and social activity improve' (Anderson et al., 2021, p.4). The survey reports that experts foresee significant change that will worsen economic inequality as those who are highly connected and the tech-savvy pull further ahead of those who have less access to digital tools and less training or aptitude for exploiting them and as technological change eliminates some jobs. It will also enhance

*Global Business in the Age of Destruction and Distraction.* Mahesh Joshi, Gaurav Rastogi, and J.R. Klein,
Oxford University Press. 
DOI: 10.1093/oso/9780192847133.003.0001

the power of big technology firms as they exploit their market advantages and mechanisms such as artificial intelligence in ways that seem likely to further erode the privacy and autonomy of their users.

Further, it will multiply the spread of misinformation as authoritarians and polarised populations wage warring information campaigns with their foes. Many said their most profound worry is over the seemingly unstoppable manipulation of public perception, emotion, and action via online disinformation, with lies and hate speech deliberately weaponised to propagate destructive biases and fears. They worry about significant damage to social stability and cohesion and the reduced likelihood of rational deliberation and evidence-based policymaking (Anderson et al., 2021, p.4).

At the same time, some of these experts express hope that changes spawned by the pandemic will make things better for significant portions of the population. The improvement is because of changes that inaugurate new reforms aimed at racial justice and social equity, as critiques of current economic arrangements and capitalism gain support and policymakers' attention. They will enhance the quality of life for many families and workers as more flexible workplace arrangements become permanent and communities adjust to them. In addition, they will produce technology enhancements in virtual and augmented reality and AI that allow people to live smarter, safer, and more productive lives, enabled in many cases by 'smart systems' in such key areas as health care, education, and community living (Anderson et al., 2021, p.5).

Before COVID-19, the most significant disruptions to work involved new technologies and growing trade links. COVID-19 has, for the first time, elevated the importance of the physical dimension of work. The pandemic disrupted labour markets globally during 2020. The short-term consequences were sudden and often severe. Millions of people were furloughed or lost jobs, and others rapidly adjusted to working from home as offices closed. Many other workers were deemed essential and continued to work in hospitals and grocery stores, on rubbish or waste trucks, and in warehouses, yet under new protocols to reduce the spread of the novel coronavirus. The pandemic pushed companies and consumers to rapidly adopt new behaviours that are likely to stick, changing the trajectory of businesses, workers, and consumers (Lund et al., 2021).

## Zoomed into the Future

What has been a long and somewhat protracted discussion on what the future of work, the workforce, and workplace might look like has been interrupted by an unexpected event that has quickly accelerated a move into the future. Speculation about office design, remote workers, and productivity quickly shifted from what will it look like to what happens today and how will it change tomorrow. Suddenly workplace routine with its office time, meeting rooms, travel, informal conversations, and timeline changed overnight. This switch to the future was not unexpected, but it was early and definitely forced. Those who anticipated future change were accompanied by those who did not, with both being dragged into the future of work.

Discussion of distraction and disruption suddenly became more than theoretical. The observable elements of distraction like social media became the most valuable tools. Those elements of technology that were destroying old traditions, thinking, and models of business were suddenly not just academic musing but today's problem. In a paradoxical oddity, elements of destruction and distraction became the survival toolkit against the desolating impact of the pandemic on business, education, health, economics, and nearly everything else. The destruction will be complete. The crisis has consumed people, and industries, countries, companies, work, workers, and consumers. They all will have to deal with the consequences.

The concepts of leadership styles, individual and corporate learning, corporate structure, and traditional thinking have been turned on their heads. The playbook has not only changed, but also been discarded, with no replacement anticipated. Traditional concepts have been shattered. The pandemic has forced society to make it work. The inevitability of the situation must employ creative dissonance to figure out the new intuition and innovation of how work gets done. This is the stark reality of change.

Discussions of shifts in global politics, business, economics, and education with speculation on anticipated trends and supposed outcomes have suddenly blossomed in front of us. The results were sometimes consoling and other times not so much. For example, in global politics, the value and effectiveness of a unified approach were abandoned for an every country for and everyone for themselves tactic. The globalisation concept took a bit of a hit. Each country ended up trying to figure out how to deal with the breakdown of supply chains, the fatal drop in demand, decreased spending, and the effect on tax revenue, along with a plethora of domestic issues that overwhelmed antiquated systems. Except for virtual-tech companies that became more powerful, the old business models lay wounded on the floor.

Issues of inequality became more prevalent, with government intervention as a type of universal basic income model. In the US, $2.2 trillion was paid directly into people's pockets. Countries will be dealing with these exacerbated inequities for some time. The pandemic and quick pivot to digitally driven systems widened racial and other divides and expanded the ranks of the unemployed, uninsured, and disenfranchised. Power imbalances between the advantaged and disadvantaged are being magnified by digital systems overseen by behemoth firms as they exploit big data and algorithmic decision-making that are often biased. More people will be pushed into a precarious existence that lacks predictability, economic security, and wellness (Anderson et al., 2021, p.7).

Another dubious impact of the pandemic is the multiplying spread of misinformation as authoritarians and polarised populations wage warring information campaigns with their foes. The potential for continuing adhesion to a seemingly unstoppable manipulation of public perception, emotion, and action via online disinformation, and lies and hate speech has been deliberately weaponised to propagate destructive biases and fears. This will cause significant damage to social stability and cohesion and the reduced likelihood of rational deliberation and evidence-based policymaking (Anderson et al., 2021, p.4).

Education was a pleasant surprise, as the situation forced the need for online education and the acceptance of technologies in the classroom that had been anticipated in another decade. The changes were evident in higher education and were quite common throughout the education system. No matter the sector, those expected slow-paced micro changes will become exponential in about two months. After the crisis, universities re-evaluated their role as centres for disseminating information. Information should be free to everyone, and it will be the seeds of cultural learning.

## Leadership in Times of Crisis

The pandemic aggravated the chaos in the world. It seemed that the only common element was that the ground was constantly shifting. Complexity and uncertainty were the norms. In these times of crisis, people look to leaders to provide direction, be a source of resilience and adaptability, and find new solutions for new problems. Today's companies are looking for new kinds of leadership skills. They are looking for leaders with new skills that can find and express themselves and new leadership styles. The prevailing style before coronavirus is quite different from what will be required after it. These leaders must be creative and intuitively able to sort through the chaos and make sense of it as it happens. They will excel at responding to markets, comparative situations, and cash situations, and at finding creative solutions. Strong intuition will be necessary, along with the ability to tell stories about the future that help teams organise their thoughts. It goes far beyond the old model that simply tells people what to do. The incentivising of work becomes more team distributed and will become even prevalent after coronavirus because teams have tasted and liked it. Stories are not just valuable in distributive tasking but inspire, motivate, and catch people's imagination. New leaders must have an attitude and appetite for failure. The lower the appetite, the higher the certainty of failure. The deployment of a calculated and controlled risk strategy becomes a primary learning tool and a strategy for survival in chaos. Leaders must develop a thick skin and personal resilience to be wrong enough before being right. Learning how to take risks and build failure into the business model is now the leader's job. This concept which was previously scrutinised before the pandemic crisis is now suddenly front and centre.

Leaders will have to redefine their roles as control junkies or chaos monkeys. Control junkies are always looking at micromanaging performance and manipulating people. The chaos monkey will have varying responses and failures until success appears. The after-pandemic world will emphasise the difference between the two styles. Because change is so relentless and wise pertinent solutions must be timed to fit the cycle, there is no room for the control junky.

A leader's job is no longer to solve problems but to create an organisational culture capable of creating solutions. Everyone in the organisation must be confident that they can take risks, solve problems, and even risk failure. Without this cultural strength, it will be almost impossible to respond quickly to the chaotic world. The culture must entail aspects of empathy and intuition that values the community's voices. The attributes the leader exhibits will be magnified throughout the organisation. The narrative, the story, must radiate energy and optimism. It must connect and be emotionally engaged with people. The culture created by an organisation's leader must now transmit a culture that creates, innovates, and participates in building valued solutions.

It virtually cultivates belief by creating a 'tribe' that believes in the same things. People tend to collate around a shared passion for community service and build trust among themselves. The traits of the leader will become the traits of the culture. Things like being aware and self-managing, being more intuitive and empathetic, and learning how to manage their energy levels must be models. People must observe and emulate the process of rewiring their ability to believe in a new future and act without proof or complete data. Leaders must model how to be continuously adaptable, highly creative, innovative, and highly resilient. Leaders must be diligent and aware of the health of the culture. They have to carefully look at the culture that is being created around them and be continuously active in curating that culture. Tone-deaf people will not make good leaders in the modern post-coronavirus environment.

Lastly, there must be an understanding that fundamental management theories have to change. That theory asks the question, 'Why do people work?' The obvious answer in the old school was because they wanted the money. Inside the COVID experience, if the government is going to be sending money to people's bank accounts, why should they work? The prior management theory postulated by thinking of people as coin-operated puzzles. Money was the only way to incentivise people, and money was the only way to measure people. The pandemic was not a good example of this theory. The government provided direct payment that had little or no impairment on employment. People find meaning in community, passions, and a sense of satisfaction or fulfilment.

The key to success for post-COVID leaders and organisations will be to build the bridge while walking on it.

## Bibliography

Anderson, Janna, Lee Rainie, and Emily Vogels. 2021. *Experts Say the 'New Normal' in 2025 Will Be Far More Tech-Driven, Presenting More Big Challenges.* Pew Research Center, 18 February. https://www.pewresearch.org/internet/2021/02/18/experts-say-the-new-normal-in-2025-will-be-far-more-tech-driven-presenting-more-big-challenges/

Lee, J. 2021. *See How All 50 States Are Reopening (and Closing Again). The New York Times*, 1 July. https://www.nytimes.com/interactive/2020/us/states-reopen-map-coronavirus.html

Lund, Susan, Anu Madgavkar, James Manyika, Sven Smit, Kweilin Ellingrud, and Olivia Robinson. 2021. *The Future of Work after COVID-19*. McKinsey Global Institute, 3 August. https://www.mckinsey.com/featured-insights/future-of-work/the-future-of-work-after-covid-19

Schwab, Klaus. 2016. *The Fourth Industrial Revolution*. New York: Crown Business/Penguin Random House

# 2

# Distraction Versus Traction

The Industrial Age is over. Some experts believe that the world is in the fourth stage of the industrial revolution, where the lines between technology and biology continue to blur. For the purpose of the conversation, this age of information and digitalisation will be called the Age of Distraction. Each age must be measured by what the culture values most, and a valuable metric to represent value is market capitalisation (the total dollar market value of a company's outstanding shares of stock). Since the time of the East India Company,[1] industrial products such as energy have come to represent value by society. Industrial companies have been dominant for decades, fostering the Industrial Age's nomenclature.

Statistics suggest that this new age is not an Industrial Age, despite the endurance of the argument. If the claim that cultural values in the form of market capitalisation determine the nature of the culture is accepted, there are some interesting patterns to observe. In 2011 the list of the top ten companies globally by market capitalisation included six oil and gas or industrial companies (DeCarlo, 2011). By 2017 the list contained only one oil company and seven tech companies: Apple, Google, Facebook, Tencent, Amazon, Alibaba, and Microsoft (Szmigiera, 2021). These are companies with more than $11 trillion of market capitalisation.

This is significant because of the distractive nature of these companies. Psychologists Matthew Killingsworth and Daniel Gilbert found that the human mind is wired for this state of continuous distraction. In a study conducted with 2,250 adults, they concluded that we spend around 47% of every waking hour 'mind-wandering'. Also called 'stimulus-independent thought', mind-wandering is an experience that is so ordinary, so natural that it is not even noticed (Killingsworth, 2010). Whether waiting at the gate for a plane and dreaming about a position at the company, sitting in

[1] English company formed in 1600 for the exploitation of trade with East and Southeast Asia and India.

*Global Business in the Age of Destruction and Distraction.* Mahesh Joshi, Gaurav Rastogi, and J.R. Klein, Oxford University Press. 
DOI: 10.1093/oso/9780192847133.003.0002

the Uber thinking about what has been forgotten during the day, or dreaming about the beach while waiting for the conference call is the default mode of operation for the brain (Klemp, 2019).

This is a significant insight with two enormous implications. First, it shows that distraction is primarily a mind game. Second, to manage the distractions of digital life and be more focused, the path must include developing a new habit of effectively managing the cognitive power of attention more skilfully. This means focusing less on 'doing' and more on 'being'. The Killingsworth/Gilbert study also found that mind-wandering has more to do with unhappiness than any other activity. This is contrary to the common wisdom that says doing pleasant things produces happiness. The study reported that activities account for 4.6% of happiness, while being present or not wandering around mentally account for 10.8% (Klemp, 2019).

The distractive nature of today's technological world with its distractive devices, videos, voices, titillation, and information exacerbates the availability to maintain focus and attention.

## Wired that Way

The human mind is wired for distraction. According to Indian literature, yogis from five thousand years ago were trying to learn ways to walk away from distractions. The challenge is the pervasive presence of addictive distractions in a wired world. Social media follows the same playbook as other addictive products like tobacco or snack food. Tobacco companies were in the nicotine delivery business with full knowledge that the product was addictive. The strategy was to create a way to get people hooked. Organic methodologies like a focus group and market tests discovered the best ways to grow the addictive market. The snack-food industry spent time and money figuring out what colour, price, and smell were most attractive. People were more likely to buy something if a restaurant had familiar and comfortable recipes, smells, and ambience. Methodologies were precise, directed, and successful.

The technology-driven world uses the same basic game plan, except it has been 'weaponised'. The process is similar, but now with algorithms that work overtime, understanding addictions more than ever before. It is about what will capture more attention and drive a user deeper into the distractive world. Sean Parker, Facebook's founder, commented that the social media platform was designed to distract users, not officially bringing them together in a social network. 'The thought process was: "How do we consume as much of your time and conscious attention as possible?"' (Parkin, 2018). This mindset led to the creation of features such as the 'Like' button that would give users 'a little dopamine hit' to encourage them to upload more content. 'It's a social-validation feedback loop . . . exactly the kind of thing that a hacker like myself would come up with because you're exploiting a vulnerability in human psychology', Parker said.

Distractions have been around forever, but now distractions are addictive like nothing before, and algorithms are working overtime to make these distractions more and more addictive. In this distraction, business companies have been well rewarded.

## Pervasive Distraction Cloud

Distraction is pervasive, ever-present, and unavoidable. Pervasive distraction is highly corrosive to personal productivity, economies, relationships, and individual introspection, and a primary driver of physical and emotional stress. Distraction is a curse of modern life. Attention is constantly being diverted between cell phones and computer screens, not to mention kids and co-workers. It can become difficult to focus on any task or person for very long. If anything, the world is becoming a more distracting place. Technology is becoming more pervasive and persuasive. But hoping that tech companies will change their ways may take longer than expected. It is better to adopt strategies to manage distraction. Though distractions are not necessarily our fault, managing them is our responsibility.

Americans are checking smartphones almost 8 billion times a day, according to a study by Deloitte (Deloitte, 2015). According to the *New York Post*, Americans check their phones an average of 80 times a day! Half of the world population, almost three and a half million people, are on the Internet nowadays and more people are joining social media (SWNS, 2017). Distraction is highly pervasive and brings with it other distinctive phenomena.

The abundance of information blowing out of the technology hole is more sensational and less authentic. Without systemic filtering, there are few options for validating accuracy. This tends to water down the value of facts and thins the fragile layer of truth that surrounds trust and responsibility. The industry espouses a half-heart effort at self-regulation.

Governments in most parts of the world are mired in systems and thinking that are outdated attempts at driving from the back of the bus. This suggests that putting the responsibility of 'un-distraction' on the industry or governments is misplaced. The responsibility lies squarely in the lap of the consumer.

What are the signs of unhealthy distractions? With the prevalence and prominence of smartphones, it is not that surprising that they can be a source of distraction. Looking at notifications that pop up regardless of the conversation, colleague, or circumstance is an indication of distraction. The habit of interrupting focused work to check email or social media is another signal. Another distraction has become so common that many are barely noticeable. Giving way to your stream of consciousness, daydreaming, or spending extra time around the water cooler may be an indicator. Unconsciously defaulting to social media or streaming services when the intention was to exercise or read a book may be another.

## Undistractable

Distraction, however, is not a permanent domain. As evidenced by research (Killingsworth, 2010), it can be reversed. There are varied strategies for training the mind to focus and pay attention, and many of these techniques are similar to those used in psychology. In her book *Be Extraordinary*, Dr Jennifer Wild provides practical and straightforward skills for changing thinking. Refocusing thinking from what might go wrong to observing what is going on is a basic starting point. Everyone does it. It is an unproductive pattern of thinking that becomes repetitive and, over time, addictive, like smoking or drinking coffee or tea or turning to junk food when stressed. Wild calls it 'dwelling'.

Dwelling causes overthinking and feeling unhappy. Dwelling as a thinking style can become a habit, the same as distractive addiction, a loop we get stuck in when we think about everyday interactions and tasks. Science shows that dwelling fuels depression and other unhappy states like anger, worry, and anxiety. Changing these habits involves new sensitivities. The key message is to recognise the addictive thoughts and behaviour and actively transform thinking. Changing thinking changes brain chemistry (Wild, 2020).

Emotional reasoning is dangerous! People fall into emotional reasoning when they prioritise feelings and assume they reflect reality. People who thrive recognise that their sad feelings will pass and use their emotions as a cue to get active so they can transform a feeling state they no longer wish to prolong. 'As soon as we feel angry, sad, scared or disappointed, it's a cue to stop thinking, focus our attention on what is happening now, focus on facts, not feelings, then get active, taking steps to make ourselves feel better' (Wild, 2020, p.158). Reversing distractions is critical to survive, excel, and thrive in this Age of destruction.

Wild talks about the process of recalibrating thinking. A good question might be, what is the opposite of distraction? Presumably, the goal would be the opposite of distraction,. however, finding the 'distraction antonym' becomes problematic. Merriam-Webster does suggest several 'near antonyms' like assurance, certainty, confidence, and conviction. In this case, 'near' does not seem good enough. In an article in *Psychology Today* (Hagen, 2020), Ekua Hagen plays with the nomenclature when he proposes adopting the term 'traction' as the opposite of distraction. Traction is any action that moves towards a goal. Any actions like working on a project, getting enough sleep or physical exercise, eating healthy food, taking time to meditate or pray, or spending time with family are forms of traction. Traction is any action of intent.

Either external or internal triggers cue all human behaviour. External triggers are cues from the environment that present the next step. Hagen refers to them as the dings and pings that prompt checking our email, answering a text, or looking at a news alert. Competition for attention comes from other familiar sources like people and things. Interruptions from co-workers, family members, pizza delivery, television, or music can all hijack focus. Internal triggers are physical, emotional, and psychological cues. It may be hunger, temperature, stress, loneliness, or even compassion that drags attention away from the task. Internal triggers are primarily negative feelings. Hunger needs food. Temperature needs a sweater. Stress needs peace. Loneliness needs companionship. Compassion needs action (Hagen, 2020).

Hagen articulates a pertinent axiom. 'Since all behaviour is prompted by either external or internal triggers, then both the actions we intend to do (traction) as well as those that veer us off course (distraction), originate from the same source.'

To overcome distractions, the driver of behaviour must be understood. The root cause of human behaviour is the desire to escape discomfort. 'Even when pleasure is the goal the driver is the desire to be free from the pain of wanting. The truth is, we overuse video games, social media, and our cell phones not just for the pleasure they provide, but because they free us from psychological discomfort' (Hagen, 2020).

Distraction is an unhealthy escape from bad feelings. Recognising the role internal triggers like boredom, loneliness, insecurity, fatigue, and uncertainty play can be the cue that enables healthier positive responses (Lerner et al., 2015). Applying the axiom that all behaviour is driven by emotion and all emotion is driven by thought, the first positive step is changing how thinking about those bad feelings can lead to distraction. Also, studies show that not giving in to an urge can backfire. Resisting a craving or impulse can trigger rumination and make the desire grow stronger (Hagen, 2020).

Dr Jonathan Bricker of the Fred Hutchinson Cancer Research Center, University of Washington, has developed actions to help face distracting temptation. First, identify the feeling or thought behind the urge. When discerning distraction, become aware of the internal trigger that prompts the disruption. Second, write it down. Bricker advises how keeping a log of distractions will help link behaviours with internal triggers. Next, explore the sensation. Examine sensations that precede distraction. Are there physical or emotional signals before the impulse? If so, go with the flow. Stay with the feeling before following the impulse. Then, make time for traction. Planning activities ahead will lessen the possibility that circumstances will dictate the day. Hagen calls it making time for things that matter (Hagen, 2020).

## Familiarity Breeds Distraction

Unlike the proverbial quote of familiarity breeding contempt, in this world of the perpetual tsunamis of information and distraction, exposure and prevalence are more likely to give way to distraction and become a habit. The basic tenets needed to accomplish anything remain soundly in the realm of attention, and innovative work requires concentration, and distraction is the destroyer of productivity.

The destruction of distraction is, however, absolutely reversible. It is possible through deliberate choices and diligent practice to develop new habits. Just as the habit of distraction has built up over time, traction can also be built. Once the pattern is recognised, and the cue identified, using the exact mechanisms that created a distractive habit in a more consciously deployed manner will build more attentive habits (Duhigg, 2014).

Deliberate practice is critical. The 'get around to it' strategy will not solve this problem. What is needed is persistent deliberate practice. Despite the presence and prevalence of a digitally integrated society, it will be humans, individually and corporately, that will make the decisions and exhibit the behaviours that will change how the world fits together. The Age of Distraction is firmly implanted in the consciousness of the world. Though the picture is subject to the artist who paints it, this age can be one of destruction or a new and a better chapter in a more equitable, healthier, and peaceful planet.

## Bibliography

DeCarlo, Scott. 2011. *The World's 25 Most Valuable Companies: Apple Is Now On Top*. Forbes, 11 August. https://www.forbes.com/sites/scottdecarlo/2011/08/11/the-worlds-25-most-valuable-companies-apple-is-now-on-top/?sh=d3526bd38148

Deloitte. 2015. *Deloitte Survey: Americans Look at Their Smartphones in the Aggregate More Than 8 Billion Times Daily*. Cision, PR Newswire, 9 December. https://www.prnewswire.com/news-releases/deloitte-survey-americans-look-at-their-smartphones-in-the-aggregate-more-than-8-billion-times-daily-300190192.html

Duhigg, Charles. 2014. *The Power of Habit: Why We Do What We Do in Life and Business*. New York: Random House

Hagen, Ekua. 2020. *Learn How to Avoid Distraction in a World That's Full of it. Psychology Today*, 10 May. https://www.psychologytoday.com/us/blog/automatic-you/202005/learn-how-avoid-distraction-in-world-thats-full-it

Killingsworth, Matthew and Daniel Gilbert. 2010. A Wandering Mind Is an Unhappy Mind. *Science*, Vol. 330, Issue 6006:932

Klemp, Nate. 2019. *Harvard Psychologists Reveal the Real Reason We're All So Distracted*. Inc., 29 June. https://www.inc.com/nate-klemp/harvard-psychologists-reveal-real-reason-were-all-so-distracted.html

Lerner, Jennifer, Ye Li, Piercarlo Valdesolo, and Karim Kassam. 2015. Emotion and Decision Making. *Annual Review of Psychology*, Vol. 66:799–823. https://www.annualreviews.org/doi/full/10.1146/annurev-psych-010213-115043

Locke, Tim. 2016. *From Do You Have 'Phantom Vibration Syndrome'?* WebMD, 11 January. https://www.webmd.com/a-to-z-guides/news/20160111/phones-phantom-vibration

Maybin, Simon. 2017. *From Busting the Attention Span Myth*. BBC World Service, 10 March. https://www.bbc.com/news/health-38896790

Murphy, Andrea, Eliza Haverstock, Antoine Gara, Chris Helman, and Nathan Vardi. 2021. *How the World's Biggest Public Companies Endured the Pandemic. Forbes*, 13 May. https://www.forbes.com/lists/global2000/#148a1e945ac0

Parkin, Simon. 2018. *Has Dopamine Got Us Hooked on Tech? The Guardian*, 4 March. https://www.theguardian.com/technology/2018/mar/04/has-dopamine-got-us-hooked-on-tech-facebook-apps-addiction

Solon, Olivia. 2017. *Ex-Facebook President Sean Parker: Site Made to Exploit Human 'Vulnerability'. The Guardian*, 9 November. https://www.theguardian.com/technology/2017/nov/09/facebook-sean-parker-vulnerability-brain-psychology

Suttle, Tim. 2014. *From Distractions Make Us Stupid*. Patheos, 28 August. https://www.patheos.com/blogs/paperbacktheology/2014/08/distractions-make-us-stupid.html

SWNS. 2017. *Americans Check Their Phones 80 Times a Day: Study. New York Post*, 8 November. https://nypost.com/2017/11/08/americans-check-their-phones-80-times-a-day-study/

Szmigiera, M. 2021. *Biggest Companies in the World by Market Capitalisation* 2021. Statista, 31 May. https://www.statista.com/statistics/263264/top-companies-in-the-world-by-market-capitalization/

Wild, Jennifer. 2020. *Be Extraordinary, 7 Key Skills to Transform Your Life from Ordinary to Extraordinary*. London: Robinson/Little, Brown

Wright, Laura. 2003. *Rat Studies Elucidate the Neurochemistry of Addiction. Scientific American*, 10 April. https://www.scientificamerican.com/article/rat-studies-elucidate-the/

# 3

# Destruction of Traditional Concepts

The destruction in the Age of Distraction is becoming quite prominent. The old paradigms and time-tested concepts are being challenged, destroyed, and replaced by new thinking. We are seeing a geopolitical shift with rising nationalism, a possible crisis for globalisation, and new start-ups replacing the industrial giants as the top market companies. The pressing question is, what are these distractions and what is their impact?

It is a fascinating question. It is not as if economies are declining, companies are shutting down every day, or global markets are collapsing. Despite these indicators, there is a clear destruction underway. That deconstruction is evident in certain institutions, as is the rise of new institutions, whether political, economic, corporate, or educational.

For the last few decades, there has been prominent observable destruction of the recognised legacy business model, which has immense implications on how businesses work at almost every level. It will impact corporate careers, organisational structure, entry and departure from the workforce, how the workforce is trained, how workers manage their skills and careers, and their physical, emotional, and spiritual life. As technological machines, artificial intelligence (AI), and automation creep into the human sphere, and as algorithms invade old ways of doing things, humans must purposefully focus on personal introspection to find their cognitive and spiritual centre.

## Deconstruction and Reconstruction

What is happening to the conventional business model? Traditional models of capital are disappearing. These models needed a lot of money and relied on a legacy knowledge base. The old playbook required intensive, heavily integrated capital and was planning oriented. It meticulously tracked its metrics and ranked its employees, and deftly deployed those systems that have been developed over the centuries. Then came the digital age.

*Global Business in the Age of Destruction and Distraction.* Mahesh Joshi, Gaurav Rastogi, and J.R. Klein, Oxford University Press. © Mahesh Joshi, Gaurav Rastogi, and J.R. Klein (2022).
DOI: 10.1093/oso/9780192847133.003.0003

New players presented themselves on the business stage as a tool and not an idea.

One of them was Apple, which is defined as a manufacturing company by the government though it does not manufacture anything. Even though it has bricks and mortar stores worldwide, all of its manufacturing is outsourced to plants around the world. Though not a traditional manufacturing company, if the market value Apple creates is compared to that of a traditional business model, such as Exxon, Apple almost doubled the market value for the same capital deployed. The current economic environment allows companies with virtually no physical capacity to compete, and compete powerfully and efficiently against companies with capital-heavy business models.

Another good example is Alibaba. On the other side of the world from Amazon, it is one of the most valuable retailers without any inventory. Airbnb, which is now larger than the world's top five hotel brands (Harmans, 2017), provides accommodations but owns no real estate. Similarly, Uber, basically a technology company, has services that include ride-hailing, food delivery, package delivery, couriers, freight transportation, and, through a partnership with Lime, electric bicycle and motorised scooter rental—all this without owning any vehicles. Old business models are being destroyed and replaced by new business models, which were totally off the radar, in 'traditional' businesses growth strategies. This new thinking approach removes the anxiety and costs from the process of connecting buyers and sellers. This direct and convenient methodology enables a nearly capital-free business model.

These twenty-first-century companies still have significant capital, but it is in a different asset category. The economy is becoming a knowledge-based economy. The bricks and mortar assets are declining, and the cash assets are increasing. While the new model has created a lot of cash, it is deployed to generate more business rather than new physical assets. Some problems will need to be sorted out. One is that accounting cannot measure the quality of capital. Valued assets like intellectual capital, software, patterns and processes, copyrights, brands, customer relationships, human capital, and other kinds of knowledge are difficult to value.

## Hyphen-Tech Osmosis

Whether old model or new model, another observable phenomenon is the infiltration of innovative technologies into industries and processes.

This is happening across sectors, with new models using it as a foundation for launch or an old model wading into technology changes. This adaptation is evident in the changes in language, with FinTech, HealthTech, Hotel-Tech, and Transportation-Tech, with almost everything having a 'hyphen-tech' component.

Companies react differently, but eventually all will be forced into the hyphen-tech to remain competitive. Some thinkers are not catching up to the fact that they live in a world that no longer exists. The business may look the same from the outside but must change internally. Retailers, for example, may have a physical presence and an e-commerce presence. This may result from hyphen-tech osmosis or be hyphen-tech creation, both ending up having similar infrastructure. The new-tech Amazon has warehouses, and it also has stores and delivery.

Every company in any industry has this challenge. The primary differentiator will be how it thinks about who it is. Leaders can no longer think of the business as a certain kind of retailer; it is how a company perceives itself as an industry and as a provider of services or products to customers. The blinding flash of the obvious is that survival depends on the company seeing itself as an e-commerce business. Understanding that the hyphen-tech element enables higher performance and return, it must rethink the business model to move closer to the customers.

This revelation can be illustrated by looking at banking. A bank with an impressive legacy of multiple decades will have accumulated an enormous cabinet full of banking knowledge. This knowledge base is priceless, assuring success in doing business the way business has always been done. This legacy bank remembers a lot of what has gone wrong over the last decades and has become incredibly careful about making choices and decisions. It has lost its way.

Even as the bank decides to modernise and move in this hyphen-tech world of FinTech, cryptocurrencies, and technology, it is much more challenging to adapt to new technology with the old processes and systems that have been in place for years, whereas for new players in the industry, the technology may lead them into banking because it is already part of their model. Some may say it is easier to start than to change.

Legacy banks are headed for irrelevance if the value of the knowledge base is recognised and used as the foundation for transformational thinking. Basic questions should be asked: How many people are physically visiting banks? How have customer habits changed, and is the current model addressing those changes? What does the competition look like?

For decades, these answers were simply evident. However, new competitors and processes have begun to dominate the market. Apple Pay, Google Pay, PayPal, WorldRemit, Venmo, Zelle, Cash App, and numerous technology driven platforms have changed the playing field and challenged the banking industry to stay relevant.

The perception can seem confusing. It is not about new technology, though it appears to be. Banks or large companies could easily outspend the competition and upgrade the technology. It is more about embracing a different kind of transformation. That transformation is in thought and is a superordinate, almost spiritual transformation. It recognises a change in identity from thinking of the company unilaterally to thinking asymmetrically about opportunities to stay competitive and relevant.

## Superordinate Transformation

Some of the leading companies in the world think of themselves as technology companies regardless of what business they are in. It is not an issue of the outward manifestation; it is an emanation of a much more profound and completely invisible internal transformation. It is a foundational spiritual transformation that understands it is no longer the company it used to be or 'the leader I used to be'. They are now an altogether new type of organisation. The remaining challenge is recalibrating habits, processes, and institutional memory with that transformation.

The legacy knowledge base inertia is evident without much effort. It shows up in popular conspiracy theories and deep-state conjecture in politics. The idea that the bureaucracy and state are conspiring to stop the forces of change is simply an indicator of the inbuilt inertia in organisations. This inertia is not because people are evil or stupid, but because no personal transformation or spiritual transformation has yet happened.

The key is the personal transformation of leadership. The leader's job is to influence and build the entire organisation's culture. The biggest challenge that companies face is leaders' failure because their playbook is not relevant.

Writings from antiquity suggest that this is not a new phenomenon. Disasters occurred because god or the gods were angry or humans had done wrong. The conclusion was usually, we have probably done something to upset the gods, so let us do more of whatever we were doing. The same strategy happens in many companies that double their efforts pursuing a retrograde strategy that does not work. Yet the message of most leaders of these companies is we are all into and committed to this whole digital transformation. Part of the message is accurate. Everyone is into the hyphen-tech world, but, personally, leaders have not had the transformation. These leaders are unwilling to let go of the past and are reluctant to let go of a thinking framework. Old thinking persists in how they view themselves, their customers, employees, the entire value chain, and the whole ecosystem. Without that transformation, destruction is assured.

There is much creativity in today's business world. It is being done by creative people and companies that understand the inevitability of change and have made the transformation. They are willing to do what it takes to follow through on that internal transformation. They also understand the complexity and confusing nature of change and their ability to explain why the change is happening to the organisation, customers, and stakeholders. Netflix used to be a DVD mailer service and switched to a streaming service. The decision immediately caused panic in the stakeholders because people assumed, mistakenly, that Netflix was out of step and would experience a consumer backlash. Leadership took the time and persevered, enabling them to become a leader in streaming technology and not join the junk heap of DVD shippers.

The acquisition of Skype by Microsoft for $8.5 billion is by most considered to be a bad deal. However, in 2011 the purchase was a precursor of a dramatic market change. The new model thinking in Skype, and later a pot full of other online communication services, deployed innovations like free and low-cost phone calls locally and internationally and began to draw customers away from traditional phone companies and established telecommunication companies. Traditional companies that did not adapt were lost and destroyed, while online communications services rose to $6.55 trillion (Fidelity, 2021). The industry is the poster child for the kind of values visible when the old models are destroyed and replaced by new ones.

## Back to Basics

Conversations about old models versus new models or personal and organisational transformation through enlightening interfere with good old business 101. It is about creating new opportunities, new offers, easy ways of engaging customers, and a new way of creating value. The old profit and loss method of creating value is now under the spotlight. Business has always been taught that the goal was to make a profit in every transaction, or at least by the end of the quarter or the year. It is essential because that is what shareholders bought into. But there is a new kind of math that is quite different. The new math shows that companies may not have to make a profit and could destroy value in an entire industry and at the same time create a highly valued company.

WhatsApp, a text messaging app used widely across the globe, had 450 million monthly active users and 315 million daily active users with less than 50 people emplyed by the company, was purchased by Facebook in what was the largest tech buy at that time (2014), for $19 billion. WhatsApp completely transformed the way people communicate using text messages. Customers commonly had to pay for texting and phone calls in other applications, whereas WhatsApp was free. One of the sources of intense pressure on the conventional business is the rise of new competitors who are willing to sacrifice profits for growth. It doesn't matter if there are no profits, quarter after quarter, or maybe no profit in an immediate time frame in businesses like Amazon. Investors have also agreed with Amazon CEO Jeff Bezos that the money is better invested in expansion, and the future profit will be much more significant as a result. Typically, the stock price has been a barometer of how companies perform, as evidenced by the profit and loss statement. This meant that companies focused primarily on profit. Recent trends indicate that this business model has been destroyed. It is no longer just earning per share but share value that carries the day.

The company WeWork had five times the revenue and value of its nearest competitor. WeWork provides office space and workspace temporarily. The core thinking was WeWork was not a real-estate company but a start-up community company. The contrary argument wondered if anyone would pay for such a foolish idea. The transformative thinking saw the world differently from everybody else. It saw changes taking place in the workforce and the emerging nature of hyphen-tech businesses, which has changed the industry.

In a 1998 article in *Forbes* magazine, George Colony, a Forrester Researcher, pronounced an ignominious distinction of calling the company 'Amazon.toast' (*Forbes*, 1998). Based on traditional thinking, the clear expectation was that this different thinking upstart would have no future in the 'real' world. Today everyone knows the Amazon brand, and only a select few even remember who wrote the article.

There is a new kind of math, a new kind of corporate capital model, and a new way of engaging in business in every industry. This new math has not been taught, nor is it part of a training or educational indoctrination. Large companies commonly instituted leadership schools where the best and brightest young people through their entire careers were sent. They were trained on how to eat, dress, and carry themselves, and, of course, on how things work in the company. The ideology was that if everyone looked the same in the company, performance would be enhanced. There was little time spent on diversity or any thinking that encouraged new or different thoughts. Diverse thinking, after all, increased the risk of failure, and did fail most of the time. The most successful graduate of the methodology learned outside of school that success is obtainable because risks are taken.

For example, Amazon had a massive failure with the launch of its fire phone. It was a $200 phone using an Android platform. CEO Bezos was asked what he had to say about this gigantic failure. He said, 'If you think that's a big failure, we're working on much bigger failures right now, and I am not kidding . . . Some of them are going to make the Fire Phone look like a tiny little blip' (Nickelsburg, 2016). The primary reason Amazon has created a $1.7 trillion business is that they have the ability or willingness to take risks that involve failures. The new hyphen-tech leaders did not learn this in corporate finishing schools.

## Rethinking Relationships

Part of the destructive nature of the Digital Age is rethinking relationships in the new business models. There are changing relationships between customer and supplier and between employer and employee. The fundamental nature of employment is changing. Whether needed or not, the time of corporate workforces made up of full-time workers was normative. The expectation was that the workers would show up every morning and be present in the office or factory. Frankly, it was easier to constantly hire and fire instead of digging into the resources pool for other needed skills.

That model is quickly disappearing, and in the face of a crisis like the COVID-19 pandemic, businesses have been forced into a new future. In today's environment, the workforce has become increasingly entrepreneurial. Companies like Upwork, Fiverr, Freelancer, and Guru have presented multiple temporary skill-set-focused recruitment opportunities. The cloud workforce has provided a significant resource to hyphen-tech businesses to do everything from strategic planning, technical studies, and procurement, and make it possible to run businesses with minimal long-term employees. These systemic changes have a powerful effect on relationships between employees and employers.

This skill and expertise spectrum can be illustrated by thinking of a continuum or line with low skills at one end and high skill or expertise at the other. It has become increasingly tricky inside the corporate infrastructure to remain in the middle of the line as was once the norm for a long time. At high skill or mastery levels, people rise above the line and become specialists, experts, in one field. In the corporate structure, that person or expertise is no longer available in the market. If the business requires high-skilled expertise, it involves hiring a full-time position. For the employee with a full-time job, it is challenging to remain relevant in the changing environment and usually consists in taking side jobs or consultancies or continually switching to companies that need the expertise.

At the other end of the spectrum are those positions that require repeatable low-skilled work. In today's market, companies do not want that employee base in-house because those tasks will eventually become automated. Those positions have been outsourced, often offshore, thereby globalising the work. An example is Apple's manufacturing workforce. It does not work for Apple but other companies around the world. There is an apparent shifting of the low-skill employment base to other companies or other geographies. It is most likely that lower-skilled and repeatable jobs will be lost to automation.

Loss of these positions should not be thought of as a bad thing, which is how the economy works. The observable trend is thinking of automation, vis-à-vis robots, as full-time employee equivalents. Machines are always predictable, and a machine can be 'trained' in any repeatable task that does not require less predictable behaviour. The rise of a digital workforce that maintains and supports the hyperpredictability of the mechanical is now evident.

At the extreme ends of the spectrum, either high skill or very low skill, the employment relationships are no longer as stable as they once were. In the 'less predictable' realm of the middle, most of the workforce will be found. It contains the corporate, institutional memory. This is the 'human' zone. It is where the memory of the why, what, and how resides. It remains the bastion of humanity.

The strength in traditional businesses was built by training and developing a stable, loyal workforce. The collecting global experience is destroying that strength. Its replacement is a workforce available at any time, anywhere in the world. They will be delivering the work package quickly and precisely. The Digital Age has destroyed the traditional model.

The essence of relational thinking is fostering a sense of community, a sense of purpose, and organisational identity that is not generic is the leadership challenge. The idea of building a unique culture and infusing the spirit of the organisation with energy is key to being a leader. A transformational leader must be able to rise taller and speak louder, to engage more institutional charisma, and to have the ability to influence the way that people think and therefore act. This begins with building leadership character, which starts with individual introspection and knowledge of self.

## Rethinking Education

The changing demands on traditional infrastructure in business, relationships, workforce, and leadership deliver the discourse to education's doorstep. Massive changes in the content and context of education must be examined. The current education system is the result of an epoch of evolution. Over the past couple of centuries, the legacy has developed an industrial language and process that has not experienced any significant change. The language and mathematics of an old industrial age are being used, which affects the thinking about the process of education. It has become a conveyor belt fostering the products most suited to another era. Students from today's educational system graduate with a knowledge base that requires substantial updating. Today's environment requires learning based on how and why, not what. It requires continual downloads and upgrades to stay relevant.

This is a big challenge not only for individuals but also for businesses. Corporations with demand for specific skills have to figure out where these resources can be found. The answers are not coming from the traditional legacy educational community. The existing system is not timely, it is expensive, and it does not produce the skills and knowledge demanded by the market. The conundrum is how to create a system that can deliver massive amounts of education and training to meet the need of ever-changing market demand. How is a system structured that facilitates resource availability for lifelong learning?

The time when students could survive on the knowledge acquired in 16 years of education no longer exists. Education must provide vaccines like a flu shot that keeps the workforce healthy. The current system requires people to leave work and return to school for another master's or certification or pursue executive education. Educational systems are being disrupted because models to meet the present need have not been developed.

Another breakdown is the weeding out of the curriculum teaching on self-management, relationship skills, and the basics of data analysis through critical thinking. These deficiencies have resulted in an educational system that does not prepare graduates for the real world with its challenges of disruption and change.

## Geopolitical Disruption

When examining the existing narrative of geopolitics, it is evident that it has taken on the grammar of commerce and is built around the structure of global economics. This language change is clear evidence that geopolitics and national politics are undergoing massive disruption. This assertion is based on a couple of observations. Democracy is in decline, with numerous examples of countries exploiting their population and re-establishing systems that restrict choice, commerce, and lifestyle. Also, regional or national identity is reasserting itself. Brexit, the American grandstand, nationalism, China, India, and other countries show the reassertion of identity. The national narratives retreating behind national walls and first paying attention to domestic strategies before playing with others disrupt the world order.

There is a reversal from established patterns. There is an interesting shape to this disruptive phenomenon. Culturally, economically, and politically, a 're-globalisation' is taking place. This involves the cross-border spillover of language, cuisine, entertainment, and culture happening almost organically. One example is India's movie industry, Bollywood, which is now popular with celebrities and recognised in China. Hollywood and the international nature of the movie industry has become covert diplomacy.

These are not strategies facilitated by governments. These are non-state actors that are subtly redefining national and regional cultures. Hollywood and Bollywood are non-state actors, as are Facebook, Google, TikTok, and a host of others. Twitter has had a significant impact on geopolitics and wields a massive influence on a wide range of countries. These are non-state actors working across geographical or national boundaries, and they have grown powerful enough that governments have to reckon with them. They have become a major player in re-globalisation.

These players' influence simply adds to their power base through the economic scale. If Amazon were a country, it would have a GDP ranking at 86th (Belinchon and Moynihan, 2018). At around $2.2 trillion, Apple is richer than 96% of the world, and there are only seven countries that have a greater GDP. (Ahmed, 2021). Google has billions of searches happening every day. It probably has a more extensive real-time knowledge base than any individual government. The influence of the non-state actors is enormous.

## Creative Destruction

In this Digital Age, destruction and distraction surround everything. Wedded to the stability of the old framework, language, and mathematics, the path ahead will be filled with the challenge of staying relevant. The important change of thought necessary to survive is the willingness to engage in a positive way. It is a willingness to take the risk of failure and to learn to listen to your voters, customers, and employees that can metamorphose destruction into something unique and interesting.

It is difficult to find a business or industry that is not impacted by the distractive and destructive nature of the world. The situation itself may present a breathtaking opportunity. Any artist will testify that the greatest disruption or distraction drives the most outstanding creativity. The demolition of one way of thinking presents the opportunity for a new way of thinking. This time is packed with new ideas, ingenuity, imagination, and openness to take the risk of change. This school of time and circumstance will enable people to be creative, take risks, think better and harder, and discover creative new solutions.

## Bibliography

Ahmed, Arooj. 2021. *Apple, Microsoft, Amazon and Facebook Are a Lot Richer Than Most of the Countries.* Digital Information World, 13 April. https://www.digitalinformationworld.com/2021/04/apple-microsoft-amazon-and-facebook-are.html

Belinchon, Fernando, and Qayyah Moynihan. 2018. *25 Giant Companies That Are Bigger Than Entire Countries.* Business Insider, 25 July. https://www.

businessinsider.com/25-giant-companies-that-earn-more-than-entire-countries–2018–7

Fidelity. 2021. *Fidelity—Communication Services.* Fidelity, 11 June. https://eresearch.fidelity.com/eresearch/markets_sectors/sectors/sectors_in_market.jhtml?tab=learn§or=50

*Forbes*. 1998. *Surf's Up. Forbes*, 26 July. https://www.forbes.com/forbes/1998/0727/6202106a.html?sh=1a9173353e25

Harmans, Avery. 2017. *Airbnb Is Now Bigger Than the World's Top Five Hotel Brands Put Together.* Business Insider, 10 August. https://www.businessinsider.com/airbnb-total-worldwide-listings–2017–8

Nickelsburg, Monica. 2016. *Amazon's Jeff Bezos on the Fire Phone: 'We're Working on Much Bigger Failures Right Now'.* GeekWire, 19 May. https://www.geekwire.com/2016/amazons-jeff-bezos-fire-phone-working-much-bigger-failures-right-now/

# 4

# Zoom, Gloom, and the Workroom

Business scholars and pundits have spent decades speculating how the workforce would change as technology's disruptive influence continues to play out. One of the changes discussed in those conversations was the concept of working remotely. The emergence of cloud workers was the harbinger of the idea and, even in its infancy, was fast beginning to change thinking about working in place and the foundations of the workforce model. As repetitive tasks are increasingly the domain of automation, the future of work was a topic of much debate.

Then came COVID-19. This unplanned, unwanted, and unexpected pandemic event did much more than increase the level of the conversation; it forced workers and theorisers into the middle of the future. What was once a unique, quirky, fun thing became the primary work model, and remote working was no longer a dream but a reality. Remote work's dreamlike quirkiness and attraction often became isolation, and its sense of excitement often gave way to depression. The early observations of increasing creativity, efficiency, and productivity were often reversed by long hours, lack of discipline, and burnout.

Remote working is not a bad thing, and its demonstrated improvement in productivity and employee satisfaction is a salient and achievable outcome. The pandemic crisis took the remote worker concept and threw a health crisis, financial crisis, supply- and demand-side crisis, and an unknown situational fluidity on top of it. Workers were not only focusing on work but also health and safety issues, not just for the worker but also for families and fellow employees. The forced discovery was there is a danger in neglecting the physical separation of work from the rest of life.

As the speculative conversations about the inevitability of remote work have become the current reality and continuous reinvention of the workplace makes it essential that workers must continually reinvent themselves, the next rational question becomes, 'How can workers cope in a highly technological, rapidly changing, and potentially overwhelming environment?'

*Global Business in the Age of Destruction and Distraction*. Mahesh Joshi, Gaurav Rastogi, and J.R. Klein, Oxford University Press. 
DOI: 10.1093/oso/9780192847133.003.0004

## Home Alone: The Impact of Working from Home

The pandemic has driven workers into the home workspace. Based on this reality, businesses are creating new work policies that will make the future of work look pretty different. Before the pandemic happened, there was observable evidence that many companies, driven by technology innovation, were revisiting their workplace plans. As the global crisis is winding down, the importance of this thinking is exploding —not only when and how to go back to the office but also who will work from home. Some companies like Google, Universal Music Group, Warner Music Group, Sony Music, Amazon, Viacom, Scotia Bank, Royal Bank of Scotland, and Group Nine Media are gradually bringing employees back to the office. Some companies like Facebook, Twitter, Square, Slack, Shopify, and Zillow tell employees they do not have to come back to the office but can continue to work remotely.

It appears that the future of work is going to be this dreamland where workers can work from anywhere, be part of globally distributed teams, be valued for contribution, and spend no time commuting. Learning can take place from anywhere and be continuous. Many of these utopian dreams have been delivered, and even more have been promised. However, inside every silver lining there is a grey cloud. This may be a time for applying the adage, 'Be careful what you wish for'. The grand design of remote work seems to come with other less-palatable ramifications. Spikes in productivity appear because people are running on empty, are more stressed, and more fatigued. A person gets out of bed, has some coffee, and gets on an early morning conference call, and before the next deep breath, it is 12 hours later. They are completely depleted and devoid of energy and wondering what happened to the day and eventually to their life.

In any other context, this is a harsh working environment. Over the last few decades of office design evolution, there have been a lot of variations. There were the big offices, then there were cubicles, then people decided cubicles were evil and there were open offices and open-plan offices, with fire, with foosball tables and exercise bikes. Now it is remote work. The fashions have come and gone, and invariably their good points can also be their bad points. Remote work, globally distributed work, and working from home have their advantages and significant downsides. If workers are caught unaware of the harsh environment of working from home it can be deleterious for personal health and professional productivity.

The abrupt closure of many offices and workplaces in 2020 and 2021 ushered in a new era of remote work for millions of employed Americans. It may portend a significant shift in how a large segment of the workforce operates in the future. Most workers who say their job responsibilities can mainly be done from home say that, before the pandemic, they rarely or never teleworked. Only one-in-five say they worked from home all or most of the time. Now, 71% of those workers are doing their job from home all or most of the time. And more than half say, given a choice, they would want to keep working from home even after the pandemic, according to a new Pew Research Center survey (Parker et al., 2020).

While not seamless, the transition to telework has been relatively easy for many employed adults. Among those who are currently working from home all or most of the time, about three-quarters or more say it has been easy to have the technology and equipment they need to do their job and to have an adequate workspace. Most also say it's been easy for them to meet deadlines and complete projects on time, get their work done without interruptions, and feel motivated to do their job. To be sure, not all employed adults have the option of working from home, even during a pandemic. In fact, most workers say their job responsibilities cannot be done from home. There's a clear class divide between workers who can and cannot telework. Sixty-two per cent of workers with a bachelor's degree or more education say their work can be done from home, which compares with only 23% of those without a four-year college degree.

Similarly, while most upper-income workers can do their work from home, most lower- and middle-income workers cannot (Parker et al., 2020). Younger teleworkers are more likely to say they have had difficulty feeling motivated to do their work since the coronavirus outbreak started. Parents who are teleworking are having a harder time getting their work done without interruptions. Teleworkers rely heavily on video conferencing services to keep in touch with co-workers, and there's no evidence of widespread 'Zoom fatigue'. Among employed adults who are not working from home all of the time and are interacting in-person at least some of the time with others at their workplace, coronavirus concerns differ by gender, race, and ethnicity. Women (60%) are more likely than men (48%) to be at least somewhat concerned about being exposed to the virus. And Black (70%) and Hispanic (67%) workers are more likely to be concerned than White workers (48%). In addition, Black and Hispanic workers are less likely than White workers to be very satisfied with the measures their workplace has taken to protect them from being exposed to the coronavirus (Parker et al., 2020).

For employers, the old fears and mistrust that employees not under oversight will probably slack off have given way to the hope that your employees are working for some part of the day. For the most part, people have got used to being engaged at some level 24 hours a day and seven days a week.

Working from home full time during the pandemic is a very different experience than working remotely before COVID-19. Remote work is no longer a choice for many employees forced home by health concerns and organisational policies. And this new reality has persisted for more than a year. That is a jarring shift in how we work, maybe the most significant shift of the modern era. Being forced home practically overnight created challenges in how people work because they did not have enough time to prepare. In many organisations, employees were told to grab what they could from their office and head home, not knowing how long they would be there. Some businesses acquired laptops and home office resources for their home workers that they had never considered providing before. Uncertainty took hold of the entire workforce, and record daily stress and worry levels emerged. The emotional trauma from stress and worry has been even higher among remote workers than in-house workers throughout the pandemic due to the challenges of balancing home life and work in the same setting (Wigert and Robinson, 2020). Stress is associated with serious health problems, including heart disease, diabetes, and reduced immunity. Employees who experience high levels of burnout are 63% more likely to take a sick day, 13% less confident in their performance, and 23% more likely to visit the emergency room (Gallup, 2020).

At the risk of being redundant, the risk to remote workers can be devastating. However, on the other side of that coin are workers who work remotely well, and they even thrive and grow inside of the experience. The key to survival and conquering the remote 'monster' again falls to a common solution.

## Thinking Differently: Mental Rejuvenation

Though it may seem a bit spherical, an excellent place to begin thinking about mentally recalibrating is drilling down to the foundation of detail. First, what is productivity? In modern workplaces, most workers are not lifting heavy items or hauling coal out of a coal mine by hand. Most of that work is automated. Most workers are doing professional work. They may be sitting at a desk working on a computer doing different work. Therefore, productivity cannot solely be measured in physical terms like how many bales of cotton or loads of coal have been produced. In the realm of computational productivity, computing things or measuring things is usually outsourced to computers. That is not necessarily productivity. At the bottom rung of the ladder, productivity comes down to essential human things—the ability to solve complex problems. It involves critical examination and makes cognitive decisions based on ancillary data, not only on numbers and algorithms. It is the ability to influence other people and empower them to do things in a particular manner. This is real productivity, whether it involves a client, a boss, a team, or an audience. It is influencing agreement in an approach, a strategy, or a way of executing. In this age, productivity is not about lifting bales of cotton. It is not about computing things in a spreadsheet. It is about solving complex problems, bringing order to a complex in a variable and variant universe, and influencing others. These things are not measured in periods.

Productivity for a writer can be in the quality of ideas and the number of words produced. For a leader it could be the simplicity of an idea, clarity of the vision, execution, and inspiration. A leader's productivity is found in the capacity to solve a yet unseen problem or influence performance in others that empower and inform the future. Productivity is not usually seen in these terms, and it is more likely framed with old words, references, and the most measurable things available.

One of the primary measures is time. How long have we been doing this? For example, companies reward employees who did some last-minute things— the employee who burns the last-minute midnight oil to finish the proposal to send to a client. Though the exertion of effort is worth noting, the employees who always get the job done in time are probably more productive. The ability to do things cleanly, review, modify, and not put undue pressure on the system is more effective. Measurements of productivity are leftovers of the industrial age.

The new productivity is in ideas, clarity, and integrating or synthesising complex different perspectives. It is about knowing how to tell a new story and influence other people by building relationships of trust and responsibility. It cannot be measured in terms of how much time is expended. What gets rewarded gets repeated. If long hours are rewarded, the long hours get repeated. The shift of focus, clarity, and logic becomes distorted into meaningless time spent on spending time. One brilliant stroke of genius is better than hundreds of millions of really dull hours.

The problem of productivity is exacerbated by the second mental rejuvenation fundamental, which is stress, burnout, and workforce productivity. Stress should not become the new normal. If Google and Facebook enable workers to work from home, it has a lot to do with their observation that it does not result in any significant loss in productivity. It is not because they are companies that thrive on ideas, creativity, and independence and can figure out how to work from home. Companies that should be valuing ideas should be valuing debate, good open, clean discussions, but they are unable to do any of that because the work from home suffers from a lack of productivity at the core. The signs judge productivity based on visible metrics like how long a person has been working, how many reports are generated, how many widgets are made, or how many things are shipped. Those metrics do not last long, and the technology curve is so fast that old metrics do not have much longevity.

This cognitive dissonance results in a type of productivity theatre. It produces an environment where the external view of productivity might be respectable, but inside it is little more than acting. In the workplace, the impact of productivity theatre on employees is usually common knowledge, and there is no meaning or sense of satisfaction from work. They eventually realise that it is empty, and they run out of energy. People like to do things that satisfy them. Lack of energy means they just check into the productivity theatre and play their part. The actors get weary, stressed, frustrated, and burned out as the show gets old.

## Productivity in the Remote Workforce

The first step in rethinking productivity is to understand what actual productivity is in the future, where the majority of the distributed workforce works from home. The beginning is to think about the latest normal and how it is different. The old normal was akin to being a social drinker. It is a way of relaxing with friends, reducing stress, and having some enjoyable social interaction. Before the pandemic, working from home was an option, a privilege, and people enjoyed doing it. It was exciting and an extension of work that drove a sense of satisfaction. The latest normal is akin to being an alcoholic. It is frustrating and a little frightening not to control the situation. When consumption is the goal, it affects time and makes the rest of the world a little fuzzy and wobbly. During the pandemic, workers had no choice but to work from home. The forced separation from reality caused confusion, depression, frustration, stress, and anxiety. It produced, in many, a sense of loss of control and made the world spin out of control.

The stress of remote work is real. It will be a factor in the impact of the new workforce model in the future. Stress is a term that comes from physics and maths. To test the tensile strength on a wire, it is connected to weights that exert force on the wire, extending until it eventually fractures and breaks. This is called putting stress on the wire. In 1936 Dr Hans Selye noticed that the same response was evident when people had stress at work. Their performance continued to increase to a plateau and then eventually decreased dramatically until mental and physical symptoms, including death, resulted. Since that time, the phenomenon of stress was added to the medical dictionary. A person could die from stress, and it became a medical diagnosis. In the modern world, the distributive workforce people suffer from the Zoom, gloom, and workroom experience. Most of the day is spent on one Zoom or video meeting after another. The only window to the outside is on the computer. The narrative is filled with bad news of unemployment, the pandemic, social injustice, and civil unrest. Workers are stationed at remote locations, often their homes, without access to colleagues, friends, or things that make workplaces enjoyable.

## Rhythm of the Workplace

The first thing that has changed is the rhythm of the workplace. The increase in productivity results from working longer hours rather than more creatively or innovatively. The regular breaks in routine are gone, like commuting time, coffee breaks, and informal colleague interaction. The scheduled workday is endless. A rhythm has now been broken. A typical working day used to involve wearing good clothes, having breakfast, and getting out of the house. Maybe it was a quick stop at the coffee shop, then into the office. The familiar routine was saying hello to colleagues and bumping into someone at the water cooler or the coffee room. Then it was followed by meetings, a lunch break, and another meeting. The day had a schedule and rhythm to it. The rhythm of the remote worker is incessant. It is a single beat, with meeting after meeting, and there is no respite. All the buffers separating personal life from work life have eroded. A rhythm is essential, and breaking it has complications.

Awareness is the first fix. Simply recognising that rhythm is essential. Begin to schedule buffers into the schedule. If need be, schedule a meeting with yourself. Set blocks of time to break your focus. Schedule time to think about truly important long-range thinking. Do not attend a meeting just to participate in productivity. The productivity theatre leads to guilt about not being at the office. Do not flatline. Create a schedule and follow it.

Learn to meditate as a professional. The separation anxiety of remote work is produced because the head is filled with thoughts, and it needs to be drained and cleaned out periodically. That means letting the mind focus, relax, and refresh. It may mean returning to familiar things that accompany peaceful thinking, like music, reading, a hobby, exercise, or art.

## Outrage in the Workplace

The second change is outrage. It makes little difference what perspective or ideology is embraced. The prevalent narrative surrounding everyone in today's world is doom and gloom. Stepping back from this opening declaration, it is not surprising that the landscape looks as it does. Humans have been quite good at creating technology and building algorithms that figure out what humans like and how humans respond. Those algorithms listen, test, and recalibrate, and have become adept at providing humans with what they are most interested in. The staggering revelation is that humans respond most to fear and greed. They are much more likely to be drawn to messages of urgency about injustice, tragedy, destruction, and death that titillate and inflame emotions. They are much more likely to be distracted by messages about looking better, feeling better, being thinner or heavier, having more money, or owning more stuff than anyone else.

The algorithms excel at presenting what is wanted and learning from human behaviour, just as humans learn from algorithms. It becomes a vicious cycle of doom and gloom that becomes ever more prevalent. The more bad news consumed, the more worse news is served up. People's fears are enhanced, emotions are stimulated, and frustrations, anger, and outrage become violence and disruption. Some elements have used this phenomenon as a machine to further enhance their position, power, and wealth to add to the melee. The effect of all this is that people feel fearful and angry. They scream at their neighbours and tweet and retweet every angry thing that helps them feel better and self-satisfied. The world seems to be awash with unfettered emotion and devoid of thoughtful critical thinking from a distance. It has become exhausting. The doom and gloom are highly debilitating and dehumanising because of the algorithmic trap, where algorithms are incapable of changing their behaviour unless humans begin to change theirs.

## Lack of Connection in the Workplace

In the remote workroom environment, the natural human tendency to connect has been disconnected and disorganised. The loss of this connection is a primal factor in creating a harsh working environment, leading to heightened levels of stress and a higher propensity for fatigue, anxiety, and burnout.

Humans share a common trait with other primates. Monkeys, for example, are similar in their propensity for connection. They live in family groups with set protocols and expectations that frame a community that shares and benefits from the connection. Extended hours are spent interacting, playing, and grooming which strengthens the social bond of the group. Human relationships do much the same thing. They enhance and preserve a civil social network that enables the framing and evolution of culture.

The remote workplace does not eliminate the social connection, but the isolation does have a harmful impact. It is not in the technological connection of video meetings, conversations, and interaction but in the unavailable nuance. The lack of physical presence and engagement affects the ability to discern the entire message of interaction. It is not just the body language, but those tiny signals used to read another human being. The tone of voice, the lack of attention, eye movement, posture, and other unspoken behaviours can be louder than the language. As a result, people tend to read intent into available connections like emails, text messages, or a lack of timely responses.

Another missing piece is the simple niceties like opening the door for someone, saying hello, or commenting on a new haircut to build social networks. They are the equivalent of grooming and put personal interaction on a more intimate and secure level. This social grooming is listening to each other's stories, and it is listening and remembering each other's peculiarities and realities. Leaders spend a third of their time grooming their team. Grooming is important. Those little routines, meeting people, those interactions, and exchanges of ideas, thoughts, and behaviours become a way of dealing with the stress. The key to overcoming these syndromes' inefficiency and dysfunction in the remote workplace is available in every human's cognitive repository. The disciplines to marshal thoughts, identify distractions, set routines that restore energy, and spend time meditating or thinking are ways of taking back control in the remote office.

## Bibliography

Gallup. 2020. Gallup's Perspective on Employee Burnout: Causes and Cures. Gallup, 24 January. https://www.gallup.com/workplace/282659/employee-burnout-perspective-paper.aspx?thank-you-report-form=1

Parker, Kim, Juliana Menasce Horowitz, and Rachel Minkin. 2020. How the Coronavirus Outbreak Has—and Hasn't—Changed the Way Americans Work. Pew Research Center, 9 December. https://www.pewresearch.org/social-trends/2020/12/09/how-the-coronavirus-outbreak-has-and-hasnt-changed-the-way-americans-work/

Wigert, Ben and Jennifer Robinson. 2020. Remote Workers Facing High Burnout: How to Turn It Around. Gallup, 30 October. https://www.gallup.com/workplace/323228/remote-workers-facing-high-burnout-turn-around.aspx

# PART 2
# REINVENTION AND RENEWAL

# 5

# The Business of Disruption

The business environment across the globe is animated by technology that is evolving faster than ever. The projection is to continue accelerating, breaking down global boundaries, changing the way people work, how supply chains work, and how customers are approached. Work no longer has the constraint of geography. Globalisation has affected workers anywhere connecting to jobs and projects regardless of location, time zone, language, or culture. This is the new way work gets done. Commerce continues to happen. The partners, methodologies, and processes will change, but the objectives and definitions remain the same. It is about solving customer problems by providing a replicable solution applicable to a market. Technology has enabled productivity and connected the whole world. Industries and individuals will adapt or adopt and find new ways of doing things because the alternative is to disappear. They will reinvent by unlearning and relearning as the only option for staying relevant.

## The Curtain Has Already Risen

Every industry, no matter what the sector, is in turmoil. Banks want to be FinTechs. Hotels want to be technology companies. Farming is exploding with new technology. Exercise equipment companies want to be fitness tech industries. Every industry is being forced to remake itself. This wholesale reinvention is destroying old ideas and systems. It is putting companies and employees in danger of becoming irrelevant. Though it may appear to be detrimental, the process is precisely what should be happening. Industries have to eat themselves in order to be remade. This is not a new phenomenon. History presents several symbols that depict the cycle of life, death, and rebirth. The ouroboros, phoenix, wheel of fortune, salamander, and dharma wheel (Give Me History, 2021) are only a few that all speak to the cyclical nature of humans attempting to remain relevant.

Everyone is turning to technology in the hyphen-tech world, from credit card companies to investment bankers to bookstores. The trend also shows

*Global Business in the Age of Destruction and Distraction.* Mahesh Joshi, Gaurav Rastogi, and J.R. Klein, Oxford University Press. © Mahesh Joshi, Gaurav Rastogi, and J.R. Klein (2022).
DOI: 10.1093/oso/9780192847133.003.0005

non-industry players moving as new players in legacy industries. For example, a legacy of tradition, knowledge, and relationship in banking can be a disadvantage, with new start-ups with technology and companies like Apple and Google creating products such as mobile wallets and online banking services which provide competition from companies that know nothing about banking. They have a firm grasp of technology, a deep relationship with the user base, and an ability to cross-sell technology. Banks cannot easily become technology companies, but technology companies can easily become banks because the current platform is technology. This happens not because technology companies are well qualified but because the older companies refuse to rethink and reinvent.

Observing this phenomenon from the outside is different to experiencing it from the inside. Spotting signs of trouble from the inside as a company moves on a path of self-destruction can be a delicate balance. If companies are not investing in reinvention, a pure technology company or hyphen-tech company will probably do it for them. Companies like Blockbuster, Kodak, Nokia, and Wholefoods that do not change, invest in technology, train and prepare employees, and reinvent themselves will experience the same fate. This cycle will be completed in a few years, and the technology side of the business will become the dominant force. The language will change from the hyphen-tech verbiage to simply standard nomenclature. Technology will become the centrepiece of most industries, and things will become more stabilised.

The effect of this transformation is fascinating. The transformation driven by massive investment in technology and the rapid ingestion has consequences for the workforce. Rapid technology cycles provide less time for culture to adapt, and that adds pressure not just on the organisation and employees but on the whole of the environment. An example is the massive forest fires on the west coast of the United States. It was discovered that one of the causes of the northern California fires was that the utility companies in the region were still using transmission lines that were over a century old (Wells, 2019). A century-old knowledge base has worked well until the circumstances change. The 100-year cycle was adequate, and change will likely be forced upon the system.

In contrast, Microsoft sent out the message to all its Windows 7 operating system users that the system will no longer be supported. The system was introduced 11 years earlier, with nearly one-third of Microsoft users still on the system, and most of them had never upgraded and were still using support. In the 11-year cycle of the software, several new products were launched and made the old operating system obsolete. It frequently happens with new products by creating technical obsolescence at an increasing rate. Smartphones have almost become disposable with the introduction of new models which change operational parameters so rapidly that early models just become obsolete.

The future success of human organisations and workers will lie in how the concept of learning, unlearning, and relearning is understood and applied. Observing the trends in change and actively adapting to them is not the key to success, but it is the key to survival.

## Co-evolution

Another intriguing effect of technological change goes beyond the obvious pressure on business systems and the workforce. It has an ancillary impact on the nature of the systems. At one time, elevators or lifts had attendants that drove the elevator from floor to floor. The same experience today only takes a touch of a button. The elevators have changed, and the elevator operator position has disappeared. The nature of almost every job has changed dramatically because of the infusion of technology. This fact changes the jobs and changes the industry and even its products.

Consider the chilli farming industry. Chilli farming is hard work and is mainly done by hand. The industry began to see a significantly reduced supply of farmworkers, which drove farmers out of business. The labour market reduction was because it was back-breaking and finger-burning work, and it drained the life out of workers with its bending down, plucking the peppers, and stinging the fingers. Labours did not want to work in the industry any longer. Over the decades, farmhands have been turning away from the business, which means farmers have had to cut back on chilli pepper farming. Enter technology into the equation, and farming businesses start adopting automation and robotic technology in their iteration of hyphen-tech.

As the industry adopted chilli picking automation, the nature of the technology began to change the essence of the business. As different iterations of automation were introduced, some worked better than others. The most popular mechanical harvester deployed a shaking method similar to a grain combine. As peppers are harvested from the plant, they move and are processed by a series of shaking mechanisms that separate the pepper from the chaff. The problem with chilli peppers is that they are easily broken or bruised if shaken too much. Damaged products affect the price. It was not as simple as adopting technology from other harvest products; a new mechanical chilli harvester had to be invented. It also involved the co-evolution of a new breed of chilli pepper that was better suited to mechanical harvesting. The technology changes not only changed the process, but also changed the nature of the product itself. Changing the chilli's nature also changes its taste and its marketability.

The idea of co-evolving with technology is not just adding technology into a business and expecting that everything will work. The addition of technology eliminates jobs, changes the duties of jobs, and changes the nature of the work culture. It forces organisations and individuals to unlearn and relearn the routines, processes, and evolution of work continuously. Another example is how work was once a nine to five routine. For the majority of the last hundred years or so, it was the norm, and it had defined boundaries, with a beginning and an end. With the addition of computers, cell phones, smartphones, cloud-based infrastructure, etc., everything is pervasive, with 24/7 access expected. Hardly any industry exists where the expectation is not looking at emails or related transactions outside working hours. The nature of work has changed.

There used to be tight boundaries between work and not work. With instant communication, the workplace is extended to ensure that communication and response have no limitations. This changing nature of work has an impact on lifestyles. This means that the rate of invention or intervention of technology is hard and fast for businesses and individuals, with little time to process and adjust. Changes impact thinking, thinking impacts habits, and habits impact behaviours that you don't realise when you get used to it. Whether resisted or adopted, changing impacts behaviour. This becomes an ontological issue whereby people who adopt accept the benefits of change and those who resist get the detriments. In 2021 as the COVID-19 pandemic had devastated the world, vaccines were introduced that effectively managed the contagious nature of the virus. The pattern that evolved between vaccinated adopters of the vaccine and those that chose to resist became evident. Infection and death dramatically decline as vaccinations increase. As restrictions began to ease, new spikes in infection occurred primarily among those who resisted and refused to be immunised.

Another part of the co-evolution equation is the unexpected consequences. The integration of technology often solves problems that casual observers did not know existed. The yellow cab business had been around forever, and few thought that anything needed to change. The process was simple, beginning with the desire or need for transportation. Hailing a taxi was also not that taxing and, if not planned, could be done by walking to the curb. The wait for service was the only variable. Successful entry into the vehicle and interaction with the driver is inevitable. Arrival at the destination and payment for the service ended the transaction. Technology entered the taxi business and solved several unrecognised problems. It enabled the consumer to locate and track the taxi as it made its way to the collection point. It enabled payment with almost no interaction with the driver. It provided the driver with unlimited guidance and location assistance without relying on memory or paper maps. Suddenly, technology had solved a new class of problems that were unrecognised. The nature of technology is that it co-evolves in its environment. That evolution also tends to drive more innovation into the technology cycle.

## What Will Change?

Technology will force a need to rethink and reinvent different kinds of work and workers. It will force a reconsidering of how education and training are approached. It will force the co-evolution of technology, organisations, workers, and the environment. The ideas about future work due to the pandemic crisis will force everyone into the future, ready or not. Industries are actively reinventing and embracing the onslaught of technology. Leaders are rethinking roles and approaches that inclusively integrate legacy with technology. Customers have become a more integral part of the process, and businesses are moving closer to them. The entrepreneurial nature of the world has become evident in the willingness of most organisations to experiment and take risks.

The future of work will involve a lot of learning, remaking, and mastering the art of retelling the story in new and exciting ways. Leaders have to be the flag bearers of significant organisational change. The onslaught of technology is coming from everywhere and in every sphere of life. It is not just one segment that is getting impacted. Everything is and will change. This major impact is on the way things getting done without technology versus with technology. The user interface is changing dramatically. The challenge becomes to participate in making history by creating new solutions or resisting it and becoming history.

## Bibliography

Give Me History. 2021. *Top 14 Ancient Symbols of Rebirth and their Meanings.* Give Me History, 20 April. https://www.givemehistory.com/ancient-symbols-of-rebirth

Wells, Ken. 2019. Steps to Reduce the Risk of Wildfires in California. *Wall Street Journal*, 19 November. https://www.wsj.com/articles/steps-to-reduce-the-risk-of-wildfires-in-california–11574209097

# 6

# Continuous Learning, Deep Work, Deep Thinking

The weaponisation of the 'technologies of mass distraction' has destroyed people's ability to focus. They have attention deficit syndrome. This happens when work requires more emotional energy and creativity, as automation, artificial intelligence, and machine learning significantly impact the work environment. The challenge in the situation has dimensions of complexity that result in varied approaches for managing performance and delivering meaningful insight into long-term transformation. Many ideas involve restructuring organisations, rethinking policies, or revising training systems. The emerging solution that carries the most value and potential for positive cultural change is leadership—specifically with the individual as a leader. It re-enforces the concept of the value of character in leadership and the necessity for adopting a new kind of leader. These transformational leaders start from a different cognitive platform. They are more flexible, sensitive, interconnected, and influential. They spend time pondering the why before jumping on the how. The key to their success comes from knowing and managing themselves. This human capacity remains a part of everyone's inner resources but has become clouded by distraction. Conversations need to return to this primary tenet and focus on practical understanding that will enable individual change, impacting cultural patterns. To begin the process, three distinct concepts need to be addressed: continuous learning, deep work, and deep thinking.

## Continuous Learning

Every industry, every sphere of life is changing so quickly that the concept of continuous learning is unavoidable. Whether it is a politician's need to learn how to handle social media, a business leader trying to figure out blockchain, or whatever new technologies appear, the learning curve needs to be upward. Whether at the beginning, middle, or end of a career, the

*Global Business in the Age of Destruction and Distraction.* Mahesh Joshi, Gaurav Rastogi, and J.R. Klein, Oxford University Press. © Mahesh Joshi, Gaurav Rastogi, and J.R. Klein (2022).
DOI: 10.1093/oso/9780192847133.003.0006

need is always to learn new things. It has become imperative to continue the learning journey past school graduation. There is no exclusivity, and the need rings true in every sphere of life. The demand for continuous learning in sheer volume is both overwhelming and essential.

Another reason that continuous learning is meaningful is the pressure to bring skill mastery into individual work and push the edges of that mastery. People are creatures of habit and tend to get bored quickly. It is not only about excelling but also finding new things to excel in, continuing to be engaged and satisfied. Humans have a natural cure for boredom. As the shadow of boredom comes around the corner, technology has provided a multitude of distractions simply by grabbing a phone. As a result, attention spans are low, the energy instead being expended to push through the hard part of boredom to distraction. Whether it is learning a new skill, being jaded by repetition, or acquiring facts, it is not easy to push through to the other side. Humans do not have a high threshold for boredom and tend to be enveloped by distraction. As life requires continuous learning to get satisfaction from work, it also requires the mastery of new skills. The mastery of skills requires the ability to have a high threshold for boredom. Weapons of mass distraction like social media have made it increasingly difficult to have the energy to spend on learning. To build new habits and move to mastery, the necessity is to master the skill of paying attention.

The previous cultural norm that education gathered early in life was enough is no longer relevant. Not just locally but also inside the interconnected world, without focused continuous updating workers put themselves at risk of redundancy. People who are more dedicated to mastery can come from anywhere, and work will travel to wherever those people are. The challenge, of course, is that workplaces are not designed for that sort of thing. Corporations have treated continuing education as something nice but not essential. Though present in many budgets, when issues arise, the tendency is to cut the learning budgets first. It is mission critical that companies recognise the value of learning and applying new things.

Mastery is not simply about the acquisition and assembly of facts. Mastery is about being able to connect the facts gathered in the mind. It is the intuitive recognition of revelations from the pre-cognitive mental process. Some would call it recognising revelations of the heart. For example, it is not uncommon for tourists to visit destinations with different languages. It is also not unusual to experience individuals, many young children, without formal language training to converse in another language. Though not educated in the language, they have built an intuition-based approach to master a different language. Without the book smarts, they can build skill through intuitive facilitation. Many have a lot of book smarts but do not have the instinctive faculties to acquire mastery. They may know the theory but not the practice. Mastery is a mix of book smarts and intuition smarts.

## Deep Work

The concept of deep work comes from the same internal discipline narrative as learning to focus attention and mastery thinking. Deep work has to do with habit building and fundamental concepts that enable the sensitivity of an external environment and the internal personal environment. It has something to do with grappling with problems but is more about developing the skill, patience, and perseverance to face the problem.

Archimedes, the most famous mathematician and inventor in ancient Greece, recounts the experience of struggling with a problem. He spent a lot of time searching for the answer but could not seem to find it. Finally, in frustration, he stops and moves away from the puzzle. He takes a bath. He sits in the tub and relaxes. It came to him in a place and experience unrelated to the stubborn problem. The fully formed, fully baked, and fully articulated resolution to the problem became evident.

The concept behind deep work is to think of the conscious mind as the surface of an ocean. It is filled with movement. Waves, tempers, storms, and all kinds of outcropping mischief are bubbling on the surface. But deep under the surface the bottom of the ocean is calm and distraction-free. It is where you often find all the jewels and many of the secrets being sought. People believe that some deep insights will be unveiled by arousing splashing around on the surface of the mind and simply having thoughts. Even if some solutions do appear, usually they do not stand a chance. The mind is a wild treacherous place with a maelstrom of ideas that swirl around and around. The mind is always filled with thoughts and has a stream of consciousness that can sink any ship.

In the 1980s and beyond, the use of a misguided process called brainstorming was the rage. It is an accurate name based on the mental ocean metaphor. In the storming brain process, the idea was to collect good ideas that pop into people's minds. The process, while embraced at many levels, had one primary flaw. Excellent ideas usually do not come from surface ideas. The deep ideas, insights, and poetry of creativity come from deep inside the mind.

The technique's simplicity and potential success lie in finding a place to tune into these deepest thoughts. This tuning in requires removing distractions and practising silence. It also means moving away from distraction and the tumult of surface ideas and swirling thoughts. Going away can be accomplished in many different ways. The Yogi's headed for the Himalayas, and Yeshua went to the wilderness. Even going into the bathtub or going out for a walk is going away. Any method of stepping away from the problem and changing the perspective is needed.

Deep work requires the ability to have the patience to handle boredom, have the perseverance to struggle with problems, and then have the silent space to listen to innermost thoughts. Most of the work done in offices tends to be very shallow work, responding to emails, chatting with colleagues sitting in meetings, and doodling. These are things that do not require solely a focus of attention or resources. Most workers can coast through these shallow things. Many people have adopted the coasting methodology in everyday life. This does not work. It is merely the outward pretence of work.

## Deep Thinking

A patent clerk can sit in an office doing the job for an entire year and, in his spare time, produce five astounding papers that would change scientific thinking forever. The clerk was Albert Einstein, who was writing five different scientific papers during his commute and his 'working' day, each paper brilliant on different subjects. Einstein's work was not as a patent clerk, and it was his deep work that set him apart.

The phrase 'deep' work is not well understood. Deep work requires deep thinking. Deep thinking is not about having more thoughts, inputs, or profound thoughts, and it has little to do with expressed or experienced thought. It does not happen on demand and requires mental habits and a frame of mind to tune into thinking. Great thinking is not recognising and assembling three bits of garbage that look like art. It is seeing the pattern in three bits of garbage that are art. Deep thinking is about the ability to tune into thinking and not about the thoughts themselves. It is about knowing which thought is good. Having more thoughts is not the antidote to shallow thoughts.

## In Practice

In education and career life, there is little teaching or attention given to managing time. It is assumed or implied that people will figure it out themselves. There is also little or no formal training available in self-management. One of the biggest gaps in this understanding of self-management is how to handle individual time, energy, and attention span. As a result, most people end up picking up bad habits. People may end up living their entire lives not knowing any of these three concepts. Deep work requires the ability to handle all three. It requires the ability to master time and do things at a managed pace rather than have it dictated by external circumstances. It involves the mastery of intentional resources and the use of energy. Back to the Einstein example, the ability to do five different things simultaneously is to master how to do one thing at a time with focus and then move to the next thing. It is not that some people have more time on the planet than others. It is that some people know how to handle time better, handle their energy better, and handle their attention. As a result, they simply get more done and become more satisfied in the process. That is deep work.

There is a nine-to-five workday because companies were trying to figure out how to keep people in the office in industrial jobs over a hundred years ago. Industrial jobs tended to be repetitive and boring. It did not matter if their attention span was high, low, or medium. The requirement was that they just had to be in the office and do whatever repetitive task had to be done. The modern workplace is now 24/7. However, mistakes of the Industrial Revolution have not been learned. Human beings are not machines, and their energy ebbs and flows through the day. The idea of using the ebbing tidal movement of energy as an advantage is not recognised. Most people show up at work half awake and go home half dead. The difference in output between people at their peak and the same person at their average could be remarkable. The idea of deep work is not about spending more time at work. It is about engaging in deep work that pays a dividend of more time back.

Highly productive people can figure out how not to be distracted and increase their attention span. Attention is like a muscle exercise, and it gets stronger.

Corporations no longer spend much energy distracting their workers and keeping them in the office. Today, workers are willing co-conspirators in the process and willingly distract themselves, lowering their energy and becoming filled with outrage about an insignificant social media post.

One of the tools to help build the skill of mentally focusing is self-introspection. It may be called meditation, introspection, practice, or contemplation and is the core of developing high-level work skills. Olympic athletes spend hours at the gym practising their passion. Theatre actors, artists, and entertainers are disciplined in faithfully practising. The same benefits are available to business professionals. The old idea of just showing up and talking is recognised as a waste of time. Leaders have to learn to become good at what they do. To do that, they must practise holding the audience's attention and practising tuning in and listening to the group's voice. This requires focused practice and learning the art of meditation. Learning contemplation or meditation needs to become a core skill for professionals, especially those who want to be at the top of their game.

In practice, moving down this path is not just about developing a tool to apply to a problem; it is about a different lifestyle. Introspection and management of personal energy involves more than just adopting the mental concept. It begins to impact eating, exercise, breathing, and those ignored processes that burn energy. Reflection helps focus things and allows for numbering priorities away from distractions that take unnecessary time and energy. Deep work is about creating an altogether new kind of lifestyle that enhances awareness of things that impact behaviour.

The human ability to manipulate one's surroundings became the human trademark. Humans developed technology, domesticated animals, and converted their aptitude from material to mental things like language and the arts. Eventually, physical brawn will be relegated to machines, as will mental work. The key will be can we remain human in the process? Instead of hiding under the bed, humans must remember their trademark, the thing that made us dominant. Perseverance, resilience, intuition, innovation, inventiveness, deep thinking, and deep work will be the human stock in trade.

# 7

# Universities as Culture Hubs

The noted American humorist Mark Twain said, 'The rumours of my death have been greatly exaggerated'. The same thing may be said about the demise of traditional higher education institutions. Even before the 2020 pandemic, the predictions of their demise have gone unfulfilled. The troublesome impact of massive open online courses (MOOCs) had an effect that was more of a moan than a blow to the industry. The rigours of the pandemic should have caused the collapse of a sector long suspected of wobbling on the edge of extinction. This, however, is not what happened. Amid the common contracting and retrenchment, few institutions closed permanently. The resilience is partly attributable to the enduring attraction of a college education and the absence of viable alternatives. Yet the survival of universities is chiefly due to their capacity to reform themselves. The question is whether this demonstrated capacity to adapt is sufficiently elastic to overcome the threats' current range, intensity, magnitude, and complexity (Paquette, 2021).

Education institutions must innovate on their roles as culture and values custodians in the current environment of these constant disruptions and distractions. This sector becomes an essential element of moulding the impact of disruption and facilitating how civilisation will manage the connectivity of human beings, culture, and technology and how they can learn to dance together. Their role has to do with how the human race evolves. With this weighty mantle, will education's demonstrated capacity to adapt be flexible enough to overcome the array, intensity, magnitude, and complexity of the threats?

## True Purpose

The need in thinking about the higher education challenges is to establish a common understanding of the purpose of education. Observation finds varied iterations of what is understood to be the purpose. These iterations come from countries, cultures, and societies worldwide and many times

*Global Business in the Age of Destruction and Distraction.* Mahesh Joshi, Gaurav Rastogi, and J.R. Klein, Oxford University Press. © Mahesh Joshi, Gaurav Rastogi, and J.R. Klein (2022).
DOI: 10.1093/oso/9780192847133.003.0007

from within the institutions themselves. Some define their role as focusing on education that will help people find jobs. Others focus on a mix of instruction, research, and services and others on producing degrees certification that assures a stable income for graduates. Some institutions look at education in a more comprehensive way. They believe that the fundamental purpose of education is to educate people to advance societies. They educate people by creating self-awareness and helping students to reflect not just on knowledge but also on understanding. In a way, these institutions assist learners in finding purpose in life. It is men and women with a life purpose that contribute to the advancement of societies. These sound like lofty ideals but realistically translate into simple applications.

As an example, they facilitate and enable the basic concepts of thinking. These are simple concepts like gathering data, analysis, hypothesis, and formulating a solution. They guide students to understand the reasoning by finding the meaning and making decisions without promulgating a position on what is right or wrong. The philosophy is the idea of being a crucible of thought and teaching interpretation, reasoning, and prioritising skills based on appropriate commonly held values. This pedagogy enriches the instinct for curiosity and develops a sense of imagination, creativity, and innovation. These somewhat higher-valued purposes become the foundation of problem-solving, another obvious purpose of education. 'How to skills' are categorised as lower-level skills. The basic applications of 'how do I do that?' build the fundamental aspects of education related to skills and capacity to reflect, think, reason, and prioritise, and implement solutions.

Of the two ends of the spectrum, the operational skill level is probably most affected by the disruptive nature of technology. On the digital and non-digital disruption matrix, two elements are most likely to impact lower-level education. The first is building memorisation capacity. At its best, this provides the groundwork for a mental library of specific information applicable to some particular domain. At its worst, it creates a font of useless information. Second, technology can help enhance analytical ability by helping to develop options. Technology has not yet evolved to disrupt the capacity to make a final choice—that remains a human role. For example, in highly technical environments like NASA in extreme situations, many alternative choices can be generated, enabling a final decision based on judgement. The risk-taking behaviour of judgement when it does not involve immediate disruption is a limitation of technologies. The human mind has developed the art of assessment and has evolved over millions of generations. This digital mind capability will take some time to develop, even in something as rudimentary as storytelling.

Telling a story that creates value require the nuances of emotion and imagination, enabling the transference of inspiration, transformation, conflict resolution, negotiations, and the art of self-reflection. This is one of the reasons that some of the ancient universities like Oxford, Bologna, Paris, and Cambridge with higher-order purposes are more critical in the advancement of society. These schools are less impacted by the digital disruption and slower in adopting new digital technologies.

## The Deeper Part of Education

The transference of culture from generation to generation is an entirely different process than the transfer of technology through teaching, and the latter is dramatically more prone to disruption. Maybe it has to do with legacy, tradition, or commonly adopted values, but cultural transference has become the deeper part of the education system. The transferring of culture, creating unique upstanding and free-thinking citizens, is more essential than ever before.

The deculturation of society driven by digital disruption is observable in examples worldwide. India has experienced the disturbance of a right-wing government reinterpreting and rewriting cultural values using WhatsApp as an army of online messaging, which some consider counterproductive for a growing society. Technology allows manipulation by people with bias, self-interest, or covert ideology to abuse cultural systems that have been tested and verified multiple times.

On the positive side, the transmission of culture normatively happens through conversations. Culture is not purely information, and if it was, technology would have a more dramatic effect. Culture is information and emotions, intrigue, rhetoric, and nuanced compositions that must be adequately understood. People can be trained in technology and how to perform the protocol or the doing part, but it does not work as well in inculcating what it means or why it should be done. The challenge becomes how the higher-valued-purpose universities utilise technology to enhance purpose. Universities like Oxford have technological hot spots in various pockets usually connected to their research function. It is referred to as having a functional impact and as being a cause of positive disruption.

This technological osmosis has led to other innovative connections, such as working with global corporations in using digital tutorials to train salespeople and accountants. These innovations have not 'broken' into the curriculum but are developed for company partners to enable free time for additional training. Some involve self-testing or other testing mechanisms. This is a positive or functional impact because it reduces the cost to the company, and it also makes it comprehensive. But how much of the learning gets ultimately translated into action when the salesman enters the market may be limited.

Whether at the higher-level end or the lower level of the educational spectrum, the effects of technology could be significantly positive or create massive negative impacts. However, in the middle is the zone where even the most advanced science can now be simulated to provide opportunity. The opportunity for reducing the time and cutting the cost for the design and development of the products is evident. For example, in the medical sector, it is the adoption of digital technologies or platforms for teaching. Teaching clinical services or surgical processes that can be difficult with larger or geographically dispersed students can now be facilitated by remote viewing technology. In Sweden, universities connect medical students working in remote villages, enabling them to access classes because the lessons are delivered digitally. When surgery is performed in leading hospitals, the lessons are transmitted to the students, who can pick case studies from their village and bring them to the main hospital (Pettersson et al., 2013). The massive positive impact of digital technologies in certain areas is evident. In other regions, disruption is the default because of the limitations of the technology, whether connected to retentive or complicated tasks.

## Centres of Education

There is a subtle shift or delineation in universities across the world. The change is in their roles as centres of technology-based education or as centres of cultural conveyance. Some universities have started offering basic courses in economics, statistics, and accounting as MOOCs. Students had greater accessibility and choice. The universities could customise class loads based on personal choice. Limitations of these technological platforms have now become more apparent over time. Education is not just about the delivery of content or physical accessibility. It is not just about getting a tutorial on some specific topic. Education is much more than that. It is a crucible of exposure with technological benefits and limitations. It is a place for immersion in knowledge with opportunities and options. It must be both physically accessible and remotely available. It must be flexible enough to equip both ends of the educational spectrum. It must equip the next generation not only of thinkers but also of labourers.

There are some significant indicators of positive transformation in traditional universities. The rise of, availability of, and migration to e-journals and literature are convenient and comprehensive, providing broader, deeper, and faster dissemination of knowledge. As the trend continues, some universities will stop expanding their physical libraries infrastructure, thereby addressing the issue of the capital and labour-intensive nature of the asset. Local universities and colleges with limited resources might think of e-libraries rather than physical libraries. Universities that carry the deeper meaning of education are taking a cautious view of digital technologies, and they do not seem to hurry and are not replacing the traditional models.

Another interesting crisis-driven observation is that thinking about the educational value of fine arts is changing with innovations like Social Sciences, Humanities, and the Arts for People and the Economy (SHAPE) (University of Edinburgh, 2021). This new nomenclature enables the clear articulation of the value of these subject areas. It recognises the contributions they make, alongside Science, Technology, Engineering, and Math (STEM) subjects, in helping to understand the world and find solutions to global issues. The previous focus on business schools and technology schools is being expanded. Employers are now providing universities with broader views of their culture and markets to highlight what type of skills are needed.

## New Media and Education

The disruptive effect of technology is evident from the media's tremendous impact, with the rise of social media, self-learning technologies, and distractions beginning to truncate attention spans. The echo chamber phenomenon is one of the fascinating ties.

In an echo chamber, like-minded people who think alike, whether right or wrong, come together and create a volume of noise with little regard for anything but what becomes the day's circus. The narrative may be accurate or not true. Everything the group says echoes around the group and creates little more than a self-fulfilling exercise. The chamber tends to move towards an inclusive nature and often demonises any voice outside the chamber. The inside of the chamber is at high risk of being misinformed and of enabling a society of misjudgement. A good share of social media tends to be echo chambers. Research indicates that, particularly amongst executives, social media has played a positive role and a negative one. Social media has criticised practices on public view and spawned pressure on corporate leaders to address issues, whether valid or not. Unfiltered noise in the media, whether right or wrong, legitimate or illegitimate, confuses and solicits response and behaviour by corporate leaders. There is some evidence that a significant number of professionals are gradually withdrawing from investing time on social media or expressing opinions.

The future constructive or destructive effect of social media, according to many scholars, depends on the potential application of regulation for the industry. Suppose regulations are created that clean up the greater degree of insanity in social media regarding what kind of voices should be allowed and what groups can participate. In that case, there is hope for social media. The key to the success of social media is in the hands of the regulators. The role of regulators must be to regulate. They must rationally and aggressively define and identify entities that distort information, distort established verifying methodologies, and create paper castles of misinformation and fabrication around unsubstantiated assertions. In the name of freedom of speech, ego-driven echo chambers are judged acceptable rather than a platform based on wisdom, intelligence, and commonly adopted behaviour. In that case, social media will not only be a source of distraction and disruption but also become a massive element of destruction.

Though it may take a whip and a chair to change the social media paradigm, some models have relevant examples of a rational approach to recalibration. The research and scientific community has deployed a peer review model that has served the industry well. They are a different breed of people who understand and are committed to the scientific community. Most scientists that come face to face with the public or participate in public affairs pay a lot of attention to what is being said in the media. They are committed to and bound by the precept of peer review. The community was an early adopter of the 'none of us is smarter than all of us' in that they perfected this art of peer group review over the centuries. Theories, research, and discoveries were submitted to the community for review and comment. That institution method has created a knowledge base that is highly validated, flexible enough to recognise and acknowledge new information, and willing to change. The potential impact of a well-thought-out social media with a dynamic platform that adopts and adapts is enormous.

## The New Playbook

The old playbook of how knowledge is acquired and remains applicable to reality is outdated. To rely on the knowledge base accumulated at the beginning of life is no longer good enough. The new playbook requires continual refreshing, upgrading, and rebooting. As a general observation, research indicated a massive opportunity in education. The global market for educational services estimated at $1.2 trillion in 2020 will reach $1.9 trillion by 2027 (Business Wire, 2021).

The new playbook facilitates the process of unlearning. The process begins with being around people that challenge thinking. Technology is a passive player in challenging people's ideas, and it must add value to the fundamental paradigm of unlearning and relearning to be helpful. This is no longer provided solely by the university community but is deployable by other formal and informal learning communities. Research indicates that the power of conversation facilitates the best learning. The axillary value of exposure to varied cultures, nationalities, and diversity of ideas adds to sensitivity, acceptance, and learning.

This model allows asymmetric thinking and recognises that there is usually more than one solution to every problem. It reveals that learning does not have one source and is obtainable everywhere and from everybody, and it also fosters the understanding that people have value and deserve respect. Quite simply, this new playbook broadens horizons by exposing learners to other voices, revealing the revelation of shared values and shared experiences.

Education remains one of the fundamental indicators of strength and growth individually and by countries and economies. Research finds it is difficult for a country to show steady economic growth without a literacy rate of 40%. The average individual's income grows 10% for every year of education (Center for Global Development, 2006). On average, each one-year increment in a mother's education corresponds with a 7–9% decline in under-5s' mortality (Cleland and van Ginneken, 1988). A child born to an educated mother is 31% more likely to live past the age of five (Balaj et al., 2021). Shaping the future society requires educating the workforce to reflect, think, value, reason, and learn.

## Bibliography

Balaj, Mirza, Hunter York, Kam Sripada, Elodie Brsnier, and Hanne Vonen. 2021. *Parental Education and Inequalities in Child Mortality: A Global Systematic Review and Meta-analysis. The Lancet*, 10 June. https://www.thelancet.com/journals/lancet/article/piis0140-6736(21)00534-1/fulltext

Business Wire. 2021. *Global Educational Services Industry (2020 to 2027)—Market Trends and Drivers—ResearchAndMarkets.com.* Business Wire, A Berkshire Hathaway Company, 15 January. https://www.businesswire.com/news/home/20210115005463/en/global-educational-services-industry-2020-to-2027—market-trends-and-drivers—researchandmarkets.com

Center for Global Development. 2006. *Education and the Developing World.* Center for Global Development, 12 June. https://www.cgdev.org/publication/education-and-developing-world

Cleland, John, and Jerome van Ginneken. 1988. Maternal Education and Child Survival in Developing Countries: The Search for Pathways of Influence. *Social Science & Medicine*, Vol. 27:1357–13568

Paquette, Gabriel. 2021. *Can Higher Ed Save Itself?* The Chronicle of Higher Education, 4 March. https://www.chronicle.com/article/can-higher-ed-save-itself

Pettersson, Fanny, Anders Olofsson, Tor Soderstrom, and Christina Ljungberg. 2013. Medical Education Through the Use of Digital Technologies: The Implementation of a Swedish Regionalised Medical Program. *University of San Fernando Valley, University of the Fraser Valley Research Review*, Vol. 4, no. 3:16–30

University of Edinburgh. 2021. *SHAPE (Social Sciences Humanities & the Arts for People and the Economy).* College of Arts, Humanities and Social Sciences, Research and Knowledge Exchange, 22 June. https://www.ed.ac.uk/arts-humanities-soc-sci/research-ke/serch-research-hub/shape

# 8

# Return on Education

Just as education institutions must innovate on their roles as culture and value bearers for their societies, the future of work is evolving into an environment of continuous learning. The arc of future careers will not be a straight line but filled with dips and rises that will require learning how to deal with failures and periods of learning to stay relevant. Education institutions and companies must also adjust to this new world. As work requiring routine skills gets automated, workers must continue to learn new functional skills. Available learning courses required by rapidly changing demands must be built thoughtfully, deployed strategically, and, if needed, discarded immediately. Educational institutions have to adapt to the explosion in new learning technologies and methodologies on the one hand, and to the need for fast-paced digestion of real-world learning needs on the other. Whether redefined or developed, real-world education will have a significant impact on the future of humanity.

As the concept of continuous learning becomes a reality, the new revelation is that the change in the workforce and the reinvention of the worker is not just the role of the educational system. The technology-driven demands require the attention, cognitive facilities, and sustainable strategies of all the players on the global stage. It requires more than just functional learning but a purposeful change of thinking in business leadership. Part of that rethinking must embrace the reality that educational measurement and return should be considered with equal fervour, just as with any investment that can be measured and evaluated.

## Return on Education (ROE)

Just as companies measure the return on equity, net capital, or return on investment, there is a logical and emerging understanding of applying similar thinking and valuation of investment in continual training and education. As previously discussed, the idea of education as a two-ended spectrum, with the delivery of operational skills at one end and the transference of

*Global Business in the Age of Destruction and Distraction.* Mahesh Joshi, Gaurav Rastogi, and J.R. Klein,
Oxford University Press. © Mahesh Joshi, Gaurav Rastogi, and J.R. Klein (2022).
DOI: 10.1093/oso/9780192847133.003.0008

culture from generation to generation at the other, is relevant in this conversation of the continuing explosive demand for learning upgrades. This spectrum concept stands as the framework for the development and delivery of resources to workforce demand that has changed dramatically and continues to transform. Therefore, demand on the workforce is in a state of flux that requires the reinvention of workers and an anti-dystopian challenge of continual training and education to leaders of business and education.

Research suggests that some people invest in continuous learning on a sustained basis. It also indicates that this strategy is not in the majority, which is adept at finding barriers to the contrary. Most senior executive leaders are pretty adept at identifying, measuring, and calculating production and performance metrics in terms of ratios such as return on equity, net capital, or investment. Even though the narrative may acknowledge the need for, or at least the existence of, continuing training and educational resources, when the rubber finally hits the road, most have no concept of measuring and evaluating the investment in ongoing education. This uncertainty about what Dr Lalit Johri, former Senior Fellow and Director of the Advanced Management and Leadership Programme at the University of Oxford, has coined as 'return on education' has resulted in the primary barrier in meeting the needs of the workforce. Mostly, asking how you calculate the ROE will have no answer. This complete lack of executives' understanding about the notion of an ROE also tends to reduce the belief in continuous education on a sustained basis.

Lack of understanding is one reason why most executives put up barriers to learning. Another is being somewhat trivial in their willingness to commit time to reading topics outside of their industry information. Many senior executives get trapped in the momentum driven by revenue and profit objectives, and they do not find time or space to build the habit. As a result, they begin to suffer from the illusion that there is no reason to change or introduce new ideas if everything is working. The catch is that new ideas only come through learning. Unknown ideas often trigger learning. This is a blind spot problem for a lot of executives. They become blinded to what is coming tomorrow or the day after tomorrow, or in one or two years. It creates a lack of tension in terms of taking the next step to finding out what the new trend is, what could happen, or just what is not known.

Most senior executives tend to overrate themselves, because success gives them a false sense of mastery that downplays all the challenges. Executives often feel uncomfortable exposing their lack of knowledge and do not want to participate in continuing education opportunities because it may expose them as not being at 100% and top of the mountain. As a result, they tend to delegate education lower down the food chain at best. The dynamics become paradoxical, with people at lower levels that are sent through educational experiences to understand more about the business future than the people at the top, who remain blissfully unaware of the changes around them. They are oblivious of the massive negative effect of lack of return on educational investment.

This becomes a prime example of the destruction of traditional concepts. No industry is immune to this disruption. What is happening in every industry is that there is no safety in the norm anymore. The satisfaction of being comfortable with what is known without looking up or out creates a false sense of security. Change is not around the corner; it has already turned the corner and confronts leaders face to face. The discomfort of exposure through continuing education is overcome because there is no comfort in being ignorant.

It is worth mentioning that a minority subset of executives subscribes to the idea of continuous learning on a sustained basis. Because of their strength of character, visionary fortitude, and curiosity, these are leaders who are not just enamoured but passionate about lifelong learning. They tend to be entrepreneurial and visionary leaders that share their passion within the organisational culture. This minority subset of executives who are investing in their continuous education understands the virtues of constant education beyond the education itself. It carries the potential of expanding their network of relationships and friendships with another searching for their ROE. These executives are uncomfortable with the status quo. They have so much curiosity that they always want to explore new things and then go back and integrate all the knowledge into their corporate cultures. Continuous education is an exciting place and is the underlayment to secure the future of business. Educated executives are a greater strength to their organisation and its citizenship role in society.

## An Idea—The ROE Matrix

The obvious outcome of the prior conversation is the question, 'What is involved in calculating the ROE?' This is a salient and poignant topic that scholars are currently ruminating on. Dr Johri, in his role with the Saïd

Business School, the University of Oxford, and his team, has created a simple matrix that begins to capture the basic concepts of ROE. The model is a matrix with four columns and three rows. This produces a pattern of twelve cells. The three rows represent impact. The first is the impact on the learner, the second the impact on their organisation, and the third the impact on society. The four columns represent the impact on the learner. The first column measures the development of intellect. The second measures the development of self-awareness and self-development in the form of character, attitude, and self-awareness. The third measures the change in strategic orientation and is about judgement and foresight and vision and purpose. Column four indicates changes in self-understanding in the leader.

The data for the measurement tool are gathered from a select number of participants in the Oxford Advanced Management and Leadership Programme in an interview six months after experiencing the programme. The content analysis of the interview scripts was used to populate the ROE matrix. The assessment determined that good executive programmes will deliver learning across all twelve cells depending on the programme's curriculum. It was supplemented by other queries like applying learnings and specific projects that were initiated. There were also questions for supervisors of these executives as to the impact of these new projects that were started by trained executives in various areas like financial aspects, market share, and competitiveness advantage. The matrix study was a joint study in terms of the client, the organisation, and its supervising executives, and the school that delivered the executive education, designing and delivering, and calculating the ROE. Calculating the ROE can be easier for a programme dealing with the building of functional skills. It is more complex in a programme dealing with leadership skills, because a single idea can trigger a massive impact inside an organisation. The fundamental point voiced by the Oxford study was that a process of valuing the continuous education of senior executives could be the establishment of well-accepted norms. Norms that include the organisations and the schools defining tangible benefits for the stakeholders.

## Creating the Synergy

Examination of the need and demand for continuing education and training and the ways of measuring and evaluating effectiveness sets the stage for thinking about implementation. As has been asserted before, the primary incentive for action is the need for self-awareness among executive leaders. Understanding self leads to the revelation of value and vision, which is the key to addressing the dynamic changes at play in the workplace. The example of leaders will quickly move through the organisation and change its culture.

The challenge for companies is that executive legacy and success have been driven by making safe choices and avoiding risk at all costs. Those choices have worked well in a relatively stable environment, but in the unfolding technological evolution, stability has disappeared and been replaced with a highly uncertain world. The propensity for safe choices has created a mindset that cannot come face to face with risk. This requires a cognitive reboot stimulated by influencers and educators who are juxtapositioned to listen, analyse, and implement valid solutions.

The culprits in this crisis of lack of learning may not be diabolic masterminds. They are more likely simple leaders and systems that have not grasped the intrinsic value in the demand for continuous reinvention. It is not just a business problem; it has become a societal problem also. It has become everyone's problem, as the waves of technological disruption continue to pound the shores of conventional thinking. The underlying question becomes, how many organisations are willing to incorporate those disruptive technologies into their ongoing business frame both technically and commercially? The current answer from a leadership and employee competency perspective is, not numerous. The technological curve continues to rise, and companies' technological transformation grows much slower. The result is that companies fail and employees suffer.

The obvious response is for companies to accelerate their technological transformation. This calls for significant steps and big investments. It is not just about integrating technology into operation but also ensuring those leaders, employees, and technologies are in sync. Experience has taught that organisations without this synchronous relationship will not perform well. Leaders must understand, acknowledge, and embrace their role and their necessity for continuous learning to dispel the dichotomous relationship between technology and employees.

From the supply side, there remains a set of business schools that have not changed since the 1960s. There are also business schools around the world that are perfectly capable of designing and delivering programmes that respond to emerging trends but have not been fully incorporated into the thinking of businesses. Corporate leaders need to integrate business schools' understanding and innovations into their strategy to ensure reasonable solutions. It is more than just assimilating business school innovations into the training and development agenda and simultaneously investing in new technology. It is absorbing a collaborative approach into their thinking and strategising. It could go beyond just structure to an ecosystem-based synergy where knowledge or scenario teams provide information on trends and the environment. Business schools design and develop new frameworks and new competencies to deliver programmes that impact the training and development of employees. The investment is not just in operational technology but also in people skills and capacities. As new technologies are incorporated, employees are ready to work with them.

The whole picture is not taking a slice of the ongoing operation of a corporation because it only tells the story of one day. The equation has to be more dynamic. The equation must be based on an understanding of the ongoing trends that will affect the organisation. It has to be based on continuous innovations in the schools. It has to be synced with the new investment plans in new technologies inside the corporation. This is likely to be how training and development will work in the next few decades.

## Realities of Educational Change

The world is changing at an ever-increasing rate. The changes in technology drive change in everything. Automation and AI impact how work gets done, with routine tasks continually becoming more the realm of machines and putting new requirements on human workers. Workers must continue to learn new functional skills, and the development and deployment of functional learning resources must be timely and focused. Educational institutes must adapt to the explosion of new learning technologies and the need for an ever-recalibrating demand.

Business education needs to be ahead in their understanding of the world and new trends impacting the businesses. The urgency of the demand comes with caution, and the impulse to be quick into the market comes with a danger of presenting superficial untested information. Many non-academic resources offer functional knowledge like 'How to' videos on YouTube or other media. Established universities, however, play a different role. Their perspective is more professional and ethics-based. The education offered must be well researched and proven. This process takes time and substantial investment.

This presents an overarching question about the implications of rapid changes in terms of curriculum development, delivery, learning, and development of employees. Research takes time and is expensive. Therefore, the first part of the answer is that education, senior leadership, and functional heads recognise that it will be costly. It will not be as easy as it was in past iterations. Past practices did not have to move rapidly. At that time, much of that knowledge was not applicable in the corporate context. Business schools flourished during the age when established learning, research, and curriculum of the 1960s to 1980s was acceptable because of the wide separation between changes. Those days are gone. Corporations must be careful in identifying who designs and delivers educational programmes.

Educational institutions must have a record of extensive research and process allowed by their regulators and internal systems to apply robust conceptual arguments. Corporations and institutions must work on a collaborative basis to design programmes. Again, both must recognise that this type of education will be expensive, and innovation does not happen by savings pennies. Innovation is scientific-, knowledge-, investment-, and process-intensive. The industry's mindset has to change with regard to how it values new education and collaborates in developing it with the business schools. There is evidence of new themes appearing in the programmes and calendars of business schools, and positive responses from companies. This may indicate that business schools and corporations are becoming more agile in keeping pace with the rapid changes in technology, society, behaviour, and regulation.

## A Non-Linear World

We all live in a world that no longer exists. The new world is no longer linear. The comfort and security of having a reasonably straight path to travel in business, our career, or life have been replaced by an environment where complexities are converging at a speed where it is impossible to do the analysis. Even if time is spent analysing the probability, it may be too late to make a decision.

In the linear world, the emphasis was on hard technical skills, precision, and scientifically accurate skills learned and mastered. In this non-linear world, the emphasis is on more than hard skills; in addition to hard skills, there are now things like intuition, empathy, sympathy, design, design thinking, and creating something based on significant unknowns, which in an asymmetric way is elegant. There is more emphasis on the aesthetics part of learning and not merely hard technical skills. More and more decisions are based on values, which are at the interface of human behaviour—things like what is good for society and what it means to be a good corporate citizen. More decisions are now based on the timing of the position. They move away from a rational, analytical approach to a more complex structure where qualitative, quantitative, and personal beliefs become more a part of the bottom line. Leadership programmes are evolving and are designed to deliver these kinds of cognitive faculties. These programmes understand and deliver content where people get the best benefit of learning through exposure to and interaction with society-level value issues. Benefit is also found in issues of common ground (not differential value); value-based ideas; discussions; and exposure to the concept of prioritising the choices. The schools at the forefront of educating the executives understand how the complex non-linear external world operates and aggressively respond to its complexities. Executive education must acquaint the executives with skills beyond pure analytical skills and facilitate the intimacy of decisions based on cognitively facilitated executive judgement.

# PART 3

# HUMAN AND CULTURAL CO-EVOLUTION

# 9

# Dance of Disruption

The statement that technology is the only cause of distraction, disruption, and destruction in an excitingly evolving world may be somewhat myopic. The relationship between human beings, culture, and technology has been interwoven since the first caveman picked up a rock. Humans have always been imaginative, and a review of science-fiction writing will provide a taste of that concept. In today's genre, half-human and half-machine cyber organisms represent an imagined state where the line between biology and technology no longer exists. It sees a future where chips in the head and hands will make humans robotic. Yet that imagination has materialised in introducing and adopting artificial hips and knee joints. Prosthetic limbs are increasingly more humanlike, and nanotechnology and chips routinely help the human body work better.

Though imaginative fiction may seem unattainable and fantasy at its peak, reality presents an unimaginable evolutionary relationship between humans and technology. The blinding flash of the obvious here is that humans have continually evolved with technologies. This fact is evident in the ways cultures have changed. It also is evidence of the success of the human race to be inventive and adaptive to change. Our imaginative nature has helped evolve our ability, develop tools, and reinvent ourselves. In a way, humans are already cyborgs through their adaptation and co-evolution with technology.

Science points to an underlying rhythm and balance between the relationship between humans and technology. At one point, need drove the evolution of the opposable thumb, standing upright, and a bodily change in vocal cords that led to language development. These physical technologies drove external technology. Mastery of fire, tools, and the wheel evoked an evolution in culture. The process has taken thousands of generations to be commonly acknowledged as valid.

*Global Business in the Age of Destruction and Distraction.* Mahesh Joshi, Gaurav Rastogi, and J.R. Klein, Oxford University Press. 
DOI: 10.1093/oso/9780192847133.003.0009

## Tech-Driven Culture

Before the emergence of humans on Earth, fire played a vital role in the origins of plant adaptations and the distribution of ecosystems. Humans initiated a new stage in the ecosystem with fire, making the Earth more suited to their lifestyle. Some scholars account for the evolution of humans to fire in a more intimate connection. Their research suggests that fire and cooking, with its predigestion functionality, allowed for a more efficient nutrient delivery system that led to the development of larger brains (Pausas and Keeley, 2009). More intelligent humans began spending less digestive energy on physical activity, and more glucose energy was sent to the brain.

Culture and technology continued to evolve. One example is language. Language is a technology that has allowed cultures to develop. Language enables humans to receive and transmit differences in cultural information and resources. It facilitates the transfer of thoughts and ideas. The human capacity for metarepresentation, thinking about how we think or sorting out concepts to be transferred, accelerates cultural evolution because it frees cultural information from the conceptual limitations of an individual language (Distin, 2011). This technology drives and is changed by the culture it describes and alters.

Another technology is agriculture. Around 10,000 years ago, agriculture was 'invented'. Before that, humans were primarily hunter-gatherers, moving from place to place following the season or the animals needed to maintain existence. As agriculture developed, immediately the cultures of societies began to change. There was no longer a need to move from place to place. The acquisition and ownership of assets changed the cultural thinking about land and borders. It evolved to the establishment of currency and trade and its interaction with other societal cultures. Changing needs drove new technology and drove the evolution of cultural norms.

For millenniums humans and technology were co-evolving and experienced stable periods of growth and success as the human civilisation grew dominant. The prehistoric and historical record of human co-evolution with technology has afforded humans and cultures substantial blocks of time to adapt and settle in gradually. At one point, the process reached a tipping point, a paradigm shift that dramatically increased the momentum of technology and decreased the time for culture to adapt. With its deployment of steam power, standardised parts, and the assembly line, the Industrial Revolution initiated a technological momentum that has intensified technologies' innovative and disruptive effects.

The equation has become more complex and its solution much more difficult. Technology is outpacing the ability of culture to adapt to those changes. Just as humans could not rely on genetic evolution to adapt to tech changes, culture must learn how to flexibly adapt technology designated as disruptive and recalibrate to evolve mastery of it. As culture struggles to respond to technology while technology accelerates, the challenge becomes to identify the juxtaposition, the dance, of humanity and culture and technology.

## Hear the Train A'Commin

The availability of technology has enabled it to become disruptive and distracting through the speed it is developed. Availability and access far exceed human or culture mechanisms to adapt to, much less understand the transformation. The interactive nature of this fast-moving freight train has three essential elements, and they are simply humans, technology, and culture. Though this conundrum seems overwhelming because of its proximity, it is not a new concern, and it has always been disquieting every time large-scale technology changes happen.

Mary Shelley's 1818 novel *Frankenstein* told the story of a monster created in a laboratory of gargantuan size that tried to fit into human society but was shunned. As a result, the monster seeks revenge on Dr Frankenstein. The story was written about the same time as research into electricity was coming to the forefront and speculated about its application in the general populace. Electricity was the unknown monster being created. It was new and different and mysterious. How might it reshape society and come back to haunt humanity? The idea of technology running amok with a vicious cycle of destruction has been around forever. Technology has changed cultures, sometimes rapidly and sometimes affording time to respond. The difference in this phase is that technology has always had a momentum of its own that humans could meet face-to-face at one time. The momentum in today's world is moving at a pace far more significant than ever before. It always takes culture a while to catch up.

When electricity was launched, it took 46 years to reach 50 million people, roughly a quarter of the population in the United States. It took airline travel 68 years, television 22 years, mobile phones 12 years, and the internet

7 years. The momentum is becoming faster and faster and faster, with Facebook taking 3 years and Pokemon Go taking 19 days (Desjardins, 2018). Tesla was founded in 2003 by a group of engineers who wanted to prove that people did not need to compromise to drive electric vehicles (Tesla, 2021). A Tesla owner with a car in the garage can go to bed and wake up the following day to an entirely different car in the garage. Tesla just pushed an update to the vehicle, enabling it to be an autonomous driving car. Physically it's the same car, but its basic utility has changed dramatically.

In this example, Tesla owners have adopted a new technology overnight. The pace of technology change is now no longer multigenerational, and it no longer allows for a slow evolution of culture. It is not even single generational, as it happens in weeks or days. Technological momentum is at a pace where culture and societies have little choice but to adapt or disappear. Technology is unrelenting in its evolution and is profoundly disruptive.

The counterpoint of the destructive nature of technology is how it has shaped culture. Think of something simple like a microwave. It is a relatively new invention. At its launch, it was a curiosity and something you might see at an exposition or a trade show. The initial reaction was it was an interesting device but it would never replace the stove. As it began to get into the market, consumers began to recognise that it was more than just convenient; it was a lifestyle change. Time at the stove has changed from three times a day to maybe three times a week, with leftovers in the refrigerator available to heat up at a moment's notice. People began to get TV dinners and eat in front of the television. The culture evolved around technology.

The world is currently shaped around the automobile. Roadways crisscross open spaces, and homes are equipped with garages to hold any number of vehicles. Tightly packed cities experience suburbanisation as people escape to the 'burbs'. The pace of life changes with 'travel time', which becomes the common discussion for any event. Dispersions meant even simple tasks require drive time. Industries have grown up around the automobile. Vehicles are needed for delivery, construction, road maintenance, and personal transportation. The vehicles must be replaced and renewed by dealerships, and they must be maintained by auto mechanics and fuelled by the petrol station. This has become the norm, because suddenly it seems like a cultural necessity for everyone to have a car, which was initially convenient but is now a lifestyle.

If one listens closely, the current iteration of Frankenstein's monster narrative can be heard around the next technology innovation, the autonomous vehicle. Another cultural shift in line with technology has entered the room. Autonomous vehicles will dramatically affect shifting culture as ownership is less attractive. A touch to the smartphone or a click of a button results in an autonomous personal vehicle showing up ready for transport to a destination. Once at the destination, the car moves on to the next call. No ownership means no garage, no insurance, no maintenance, and no refuelling. Cities will not need space for parking and there will not be the necessity to spend large amounts of money on road maintenance as the number of vehicles will decline significantly. Patterns of homeownership may change as consumers no longer have the limitations of auto ownership. Suddenly, society changes again, as it does with every invention, initiative, and innovation. Culture becomes the buffer between humans and technology.

## New Process and Productive Patterns

The cultural buffer between humans and technology allows space to find meaning in the technology and define purpose in the society. Culture cannot move fast enough into the future because the patterns are always new. At face value, the modern era is full of destruction, and distractions have some commonality with all those other 'destruction and distraction' times. Examining history can provide a framework and thinking and tools to reclaim the balance between fast-changing technology and humans.

There was a time that a lot of cultural value was put on the importance of having good handwriting. The culture demanded compliance with existing technology; therefore, because writing a letter was a primary communication mechanism, the writer's penmanship sent a message as important as the letter's content. The style of handwriting was important. And good handwriting probably depicted your personality, how well organised you are, and how well you write. The new technology has removed that pressure on handwriting and replaced it with the importance of structure and form. Fast computers, smartphones, emails, and text messages have replaced handwritten letters, but the same constructive patterns can be applied to the new communication technology.

This is not a reversion of an older culture but the application of previously established and successful patterns. Just as technology has its momentum independent of human ability to drive it, this is true of ideas—they have their own momentum. Previous cultural patterns are useful because there are stable patterns that connect to the essential humanity of imagination and innovation.

To illustrate this, take the example of the banking system. The world of commerce has seen numerous iterations over time. It has moved from a simple bartering system to a currency system and now to cashless transactions. The development of trade and commerce drove the institution of banking; it was a methodology, a system, of how currency could be traded and exchanged worldwide. Technology has made the value of transactions and the stability of an accepted process its currency. The same hyphen-tech that made the banking system is the largest disruptive agent threatening the banking industry. This new cultural evolution can be met with resistance or strategic patterns. Learning from the past will improve the culture, and not learning will obliterate it.

Science-fiction writers often use older cultures as a reference for projecting the future. Curiously, science-fiction writers often get it right for that exact reason. It is important to remember that technology changes things, but it is also changing. The prevailing thinking is that because technology is changing, everything will be different. Reality reveals that basic humanity is not changing. It remains the connective bridge from technology to culture. Therefore, previous connections stay valid.

## Two Strategies

Amidst an age of massive destruction of ideas and institutions once considered bastions of order and stability, watching them despairingly crumble along with businesses, economics, individual relationships, and education models is discomforting. Add to this the massive distraction that technology is capable of, and most would probably like to hide under the bed. If history teaches any lessons, the normative human response is to think about being under the bed but realising that, 'The important work of moving the world forward does not wait to be done by perfect men (people)' (Eliot, 2021).

The examination of how society responds to change is complex and confusing. However, in its simplest form, it involves two basic strategies: an inside and an outside strategy. The internal strategy has to do with control of individual thought, passion, and behaviour. The first examination is internal introspection, which helps leaders of all shapes and sizes identify what is important, what is valued, and what the priorities are. It becomes an examination of character and builds clarity and confidence in understanding individual identity and position in the continuum of life. It is this basic exercise that builds the foundation of action. It translates as passion and confidence that enables influence and motivation for others. It is the key to successful leadership.

The external strategy stands on the shoulders of the first strategy. It allows leaders to exhibit the wisdom of ages of leaders who have called for a version of the truth in previous cultures and civilisations. It will enable people to be more grounded in themselves and influences them to find meaning in activity, irrespective of the outcomes, that allows them to derive meaning from action and not possessions. It encourages sensitivity and diversity and fosters interaction that seeks common ground. It is interactive and aggressive in presenting culturally adopted values that promote involvement and influence participation in the community. This approach represents cultural norms that have been stable for millenniums. It is the primary conversation that will facilitate meaningful change in cultures. It positions leaders as the leading partner in the dance with disruption.

## Bibliography

Desjardins, Jeff. 2018. How Long Does It Take to Hit 50 Million Users? Visual Capitalist, 8 June. https://www.visualcapitalist.com/how-long-does-it-take-to-hit-50-million-users/

Distin, Kate. 2011. Cultural Evolution. Cambridge: Cambridge University Press

Eliot, George. 2021. George Eliot Quotes. Brainy Quotes, 24 June. https://www.brainyquote.com/quotes/george_eliot_148930

Pausas, Juli, and Jon Keeley. 2009. A Burning Story: The Role of Fire in the History of Life. *BioScience, American Institute of Biological Sciences*, Vol. 59, Issue 7:593–601

Tesla. 2021. Tesla's Mission Is to Accelerate the World's Transition to Sustainable Energy. Tesla, 24 June. https://www.tesla.com/about

# 10

# Keeping Sane in Insane Times

In the Land's End area of San Francisco, there are more than three hundred sunken ships, three of which are still visible. At high tide they are invisible, but as the tide goes out the shipwrecks are visible in their entirety (Atlas Obscura, 2021). Something similar happens in the personal and professional lives of leaders and workers. In the Age of Destruction and Distraction, everything has changed. With the arrival of the COVID-19 crisis, those changes rearranged the furniture and the way work got done. But at its essence, everything still looked pretty much the same. Leaders were forced to rethink, workers became remote, but the work was still the work. With its isolation and its lack of schedule, routine, personal interaction, commuting, bookended days, and separation of personal and professional time, the tide of crisis has exposed the wrecks. It has revealed the shipwreck of discipline, energy, introspection, and burnout. Remote workers wake up in the morning and get on the first call. There is no commute and nothing bookends the day and separates personal and professional life. There is no personal contact with people and a lack of clarity about what is happening in the world during crises. It is easy to experience uncertainty in a remote environment, with the repetition of the cycle day after week after month. There is little variety, connection, and focus, alienating energy activity and becoming a sure-fire recipe for burnout.

The challenge of dealing with the wreck is not new but has been around forever. These wrecks were not caused by the low tide but have always been under the surface. People have been candidates for burnout forever. The coronavirus crisis has exposed the lack of connection, variety, routine, and bookended days, and the inability to connect with personal and spiritual sources of energy that have been perennial problems. Because of the predominance of the problem, there are some salient solutions. Examination of them is not part of the everyday dialogue tools or methodologies and they are seldom systematically explored at great length. This nuanced conversation deals with building routines and identifying sources and methods of personal energy. It explores the value of introspection

*Global Business in the Age of Destruction and Distraction.* Mahesh Joshi, Gaurav Rastogi, and J.R. Klein, Oxford University Press. © Mahesh Joshi, Gaurav Rastogi, and J.R. Klein (2022).
DOI: 10.1093/oso/9780192847133.003.0010

or meditation as a mind cleaner and the delicate topic of personal belief systems and spirituality.

## Routine

Humans are creatures of habit. Chinese Taoism believes that if any task is repeated for too long, fatigue sets in and energy levels drop, resulting in a drop in activity. There is nothing in the material world that can be repeated forever. Even high-level performance, if taken to the extreme, becomes detrimental. The issue is that the lack of variety saps energy. Intense activities require break periods. This is true not just of humans but is also how nature works. Farmers across the globe have understood the value of allowing land to lay fallow periodically, and land that rests periodically produces better.

Building a routine builds habits and tools that will manage energy and hence performance. Especially in remote work, it is natural to think that focused effort maximises performance, but in reality, that is not practical or beneficial. The energy payoff is low, and creativity, interaction, and coherent thinking are quickly lost. Breaks can take various forms, both passive and active. Passive activities have a low energy payoff. Things like watching television, eating, or social media crawling can be energy vampires that add to the problem. Activities like physical exercise, social interaction, going outside, or group activity like yoga can be energy sources and perfect breaks from work.

'Having a routine not only guides you through your days, but it also brings mental and physical benefits, too, whether by adding exercise to your day, aiding in getting better sleep, helping children feel more secure or providing a sense of control during such an uncertain time' (Petri, 2020).

By establishing a daily routine, time can be set aside to take care of tasks and focus on our mental and physical health. Routines are essential at every stage of life—from childhood and adolescence to adulthood. They help cope with change, create healthy habits, improve interpersonal relationships, and reduce stress. Studies have shown that daily routines have far-reaching mental health benefits—from alleviating bipolar disorder and preventing substance abuse to managing the symptoms of other mental illnesses. It takes 21 days to form a new habit, and the same goes for a routine. If you set and stick to a new plan for three weeks, there's a good chance you'll stick to the pattern for a long time.

Routines help alleviate anxiety. It is essential to sit down, identify what's worrying you, and address your concerns to cope with stress. When we create daily routines by exercising or changing our sleeping patterns, our bodies can adjust and know what to expect. The same goes for mental routines. Creating predictable scenarios through habits allows your mind to adjust, understand what to expect, and alleviate anxiety over the unknown. Journaling is a great way to establish a regular schedule, especially for those struggling with anxiety disorder symptoms. Journaling at the same time every day can help start a process, or routine, of mental restoration and wellness. Routines promote healthy habits. For people with busy schedules, daily plans can promote healthy lifestyle habits. Simple changes like packing your lunch before work can help you eat a more balanced diet, while going to bed at the same time every night can promote a consistent sleep schedule (Therapy Group of NYC, 2021).

Additionally, set aside time to focus on your physical health. You don't need to spend hours in the gym every day to enjoy the benefits of exercise. If time is short, scheduling a few minutes of high-intensity interval training (HIIT) can boost self-esteem, improve mood, and provide numerous mental health benefits, according to the National Institute of Mental Health. Routines help combat burnout. According to a national survey on behavioural health, one-third of adults in the United States experienced extreme stress within the past year. In contrast, nearly half of adults believe their stress levels increased over the past year. The gradual accumulation of stress leads to burnout, which can cause mental and emotional exhaustion, poor interpersonal relationships, and lost productivity at work. While it affects everyone differently, burnout can lead to serious health conditions and mental health issues over time (Therapy Group of NYC, 2021).

## Meditation

One of the primary things for professionals interested in performing well, staying active, and being employed is learning to reflect on self or meditate. Multitasking is a favourite pastime of many professionals. It provides a false assumption of efficiency and effective performance. Research indicates that, especially in working remotely, too many tasks at one time causes attention residue. Every point of attention, focus, and activity takes a little energy, physical and mental, that enables the potential for maximum performance. The day may begin with a hundred units of energy and every bit of attention, whether productive work, social media, phone calls, the stock market, or jumping from focus to focus. As the drain continues, mental capacity decreases because it is clogged with all types of attention, whether they make sense or are nonsense. The result is lowered attention span and lower ability to comprehend complexities. The conscious mind can handle only a few things at a time, and attention residue saps energy and decreases the ability to process anything deeper than at the surface level. The mental noises with their many voices vie for prominence. At the core, thoughts like intuition, creativity, and clarity get pushed beneath the clutter. As residue accumulates and energy dissipates, access to clarity is lost. Executives are always racing against time, with the logical assumption that being short of time creates the paradox of playing against yourself.

The key to control over attention is introspection. Learning to contemplate, reflect, or meditate allows for cleansing mental consciousness. Yoga calls it warping of consciousness. It is meant to clean up the clutter and move back to a clean slate. It is essential for professionals because of the complexity necessary from what happened 20 meetings ago to what happened 20 years ago, with all the intricacies attached. For leaders, learning to meditate is their superpower. It is the ability to reclaim power over attention. Once reclaimed, it facilitates new growth and nuance that allows clarity in direction and wisdom in execution.

Learning to meditate and be introspective connects to the deeper resources available to humans. Computers will continue to get better at doing everything. Machines are better at lifting things and computing things than humans. They will become ever more adept at handling complex items and decisions. However, they will struggle with the elemental human realms of intuition, clarity, purpose, and influence. These things all require the ability to have control of our attention.

## Spiritual Energy

Energy can be defined as the ability to move around. There are two primary forms of energy: kinetic energy and potential energy. Kinetic energy is the energy in moving objects or mass. Potential energy is any form of energy that has been stored and potentially put to future use (Vikaspedia, 2021). Energy is not just a physical function but is also mental. Getting mentally energised to achieve a goal creates physiological energy. That energy is reflected both in a change in blood pressure and an increased ability to perform a physical task. Mental energy creates a physiological and physical response (Markman, 2014). It is this physiological energy that provides the ability not only to engage in thinking but also to apply willpower to an activity. This energy drives the organisation of routine and the discipline of meditation. It is also the foundation for spiritual energy.

Spiritual energy is the most profound source of energy driving human behaviour, and it feeds motivation and momentum. The Age of Disruption is filled with distraction vampires that spew negativity and feed on fear and greed. The continual narrative that danger is coming to the neighbourhood, the home, the head, the feet, the lungs occurs because the algorithms were designed to feed the user fears. People are feeding on their fear and have become accustomed to it, and it has become a significant drain on energy. Scientists and theologists agree that the world is collapsing, but not just yet.

Another thing that saps energy is work avoidance—explicitly, avoiding the work that we know needs to be done but not just yet. Procrastination takes up a lot of energy because a cyclical cognitive load is required in regurgitation, and rumination on avoidance rationale becomes costly. Work avoidance is a mental energy issue with an obvious solution: get the work done now. The solution payment results in a payback immediately. Completing a job gives a good feeling that builds energy, simply requiring willpower.

Human existence has physical energy, mental energy, and willpower and spiritual energy sources. An interesting observation is that payback energy activities feed all sources at once. An example is the ability to serve other people. Humans are a social species designed to live in packs and groups, which has evolved into the way society works. The community is designed to serve each other. Without this, there is no structured way for humanity to survive. Some ideological communities have programmes to teach adherents how to serve, but ideas, beliefs, and willpower drive most service. People who service feel better, not because they are superior but because they are designed to serve, and when doing so they receive a big energy payoff—they feel good. It becomes a break in the routine and connection with other people, a means of expression and inner exploration that can provide continual energy payback.

Willpower, serving others, and intentional introspection all have a foundation in routines, practices, and systems of belief. Whether religious or non-religious, whether spiritual or unspiritual, it is clear that people behave as they believe. In the 1980s, people on Wall Street were called masters of the universe. But life's revelation of reality is obvious. Regardless of nomenclature, humans have little control over forces beyond their control. It is also evident that existence has much larger and more complex forces at play. Humans are at the margin of these forces and only experience the interaction between pressures.

The question is one of defining the nature of the relationship with that source of energy, logic, entity, or intuition that drives the entire universe. Common wisdom speculates that we are all masters of our fate, but reality reveals that we have no control over anything. If so, there would be no frustration, pandemic, or discomfort. How does this conversation fit into a professional setting? The answer is that a lot of energy is lost while trying to control the universe. It is like gambling; the house always wins. There is no way to win against the 'will' of the universe, and therefore the fight is wasted energy. It is wiser to spend time and energy understanding what role in the scheme of things brings relevance. Personal routine, meditation practices, serving other people, and becoming conscious of the movement of energy in the community and the individual defines a personal place in the universe. That cognitive introspection changes character and drives behaviour.

Spending time building a wall against a tsunami of the inevitable is pointless. Instead of wasting energy building a wall, the same energy can be deployed securing against the vicissitudes of the future and understanding that walls have not worked well throughout history. As flawed as they may be, the traditional systems of thought and religion have inculcated the basic concepts of surrendering the ego, practising routines, servicing the community, and daily practice that has sustained humanity.

This exertion of willpower will reveal that the larger forces are not antithetical. The nature of the relationship with the universe is not enmity; the relationship is one of friendliness, kindness, and tenderness of connection. Once realised, the relationship becomes a source of energy, and life becomes more comfortable. Winning or losing, success or failure no longer matters.

## Bibliography

Atlas Obscura. 2021. The Shipwrecks at Land's End. Atlas Obscura: July 23. https://www.atlasobscura.com/places/shipwrecks-lands-end

Markman, Art. 2014. Mental Energy and Physiological Energy. Psychology Today, 12 February. https://www.psychologytoday.com/us/blog/ulterior-motives/201402/mental-energy-and-physiological-energy

Petri, Alexandra E. 2020. Benefit From a Fall Routine. *The New York Times*, 5 September. https://www.nytimes.com/2020/09/05/at-home/benefit-from-a-fall-routine.html

Therapy Group of NYC. 2021. The Mental Health Benefits of Having a Daily Routine. Therapy Group of NYC, 23 July. https://nyctherapy.com/therapists-nyc-blog/the-mental-health-benefits-of-having-a-daily-routine/

Vikaspedia. 2021. Forms of Energy. Vikaspedia, 23 July. https://vikaspedia.in/energy/energy-basics/forms-of-energy

# 11

# The Failure Gym

Disruptions and distractions become the two-edged sword of change. At first blush, it seems to be the destruction of worlds in its relentless onslaught of attention-capturing additions. Companies and institutions that have been the bastions of culture, society, and civilisation are drowning in the flood of technology. Highly revered legacy ideas and traditions long considered the fundamental foundation of success have crumbled, becoming irrelevant and many times barriers. Every sector must deal with the annihilation of business models that thrived in stable times and must struggle with traditional thinking to cope with new math and tectonic shifts in business, health, education, and government.

Workers that have learned skills and built capacities to last a life find it perplexing, confusing, and frightening that job requirements have moved away from their strengths. They see jobs once considered careers taken over by automation. The technological upgrade of the workplace, shop floor, classroom, and manufacturing plants has made jobs disappear.

Employers in every sector are grappling with new business models filled with technologies, strategies, and fallacies that challenge the comfort of traditions. They are witnessing the transformation of processes and products, how the work gets done, and who does it. Their workforce requirements continue to change within a cycle of digital change. The relic of hiring a stable of labourers to perform repetitive processes is steadily disappearing and being replaced by a mechanical workforce that requires no benefits or time off. Changing skill demand is moving to a cloud workforce with no geographic limitations. Leaders, employer, and employees face the challenge of coping with these changes and accepting the realisation that this is the new normal.

However, the other edge of the sword has opened a vista filled with opportunity. Change always comes with a bit of pain. Most resist it because it hurts too much to make the change. That reticence is maintained until it hurts less to change than it does to remain the same. It turns out that humans have not changed that much over their existence. Faced with something different or unknown, the fight or flight response is involuntary. The

*Global Business in the Age of Destruction and Distraction.* Mahesh Joshi, Gaurav Rastogi, and J.R. Klein, Oxford University Press. 
DOI: 10.1093/oso/9780192847133.003.0011

response is an automatic physiological reaction to an event perceived as stressful or frightening. The perception of threat activates the sympathetic nervous system and triggers an acute stress response that prepares the body to fight or flee. These responses are evolutionary adaptations to increase the chances of survival in threatening situations. Overly frequent, intense, or inappropriate activation of the fight or flight response is implicated in various clinical conditions, including most anxiety disorders (Psychology Tools, 2021).

The fight or flight physiology feeds directly into emotional processing, and its effect is to bring about immediate behaviour. Though humans still deal with the same basic physiology, they have developed a mental capacity that allows control or management of the emotional component. The tool of thinking still enables the same function. Change is that stressful frightening event and solicits that same response. Facing change becomes a learned and purposeful process. Humanity is again faced with disruptive technological change that will produce four basic reactions. These reactions are much like reactions experienced in the grieving process.

The first is denial. It usually is observed as soon as a change is implemented. Even if the signs of change are undeniable, the narrative will deny that it arrived. It is driven by the fear of losing a sense of belonging, safety, and psychological needs. To escape the ominous feeling, the importance of change is rejected.

The second reaction is resistance. The resisters recognise and accept the change but not with open arms. Their narrative clarifies that the change is not wanted, and they will actively work to keep it from happening. It is filled with attempts to switch back to the old ways of doing things, finding any minutiae that are wrong or problematic, and complaints. Resisters often criticise, blame, and respond with anger.

Number three is exploration. This stage often follows unsuccessful resistance and acknowledges that the change cannot be stopped. It sparks the curiosity to explore the change and identify a place to fit into the new system. This step may result in scepticism leading to exploration of alternatives but is mostly hopeful about the change.

The final reaction is acceptance, whether at the end of a process or the beginning. Thoughtful acceptance is evidenced by active commitment to making it work and wilfully integrating it into the processes, thinking, and values involved. The blinding flash of the obvious is that the process, though necessary and vital, only delivers the participant to the front step of the challenge of coping with the changes. It is the point where introspection, attention, self-understanding, and cognitive facilities decide to head back to the cave or face the world and be part of history.

## New Forms of Power

Technology is creating new ways to interact as a society. Humanity, culture, and technology have always co-evolved. New human technology like the opposable thumb, a bigger prefrontal cortex, or the ability to stand upright has evolved slowly. Cultural evolution has been quicker with language development, the wheel, agriculture, and creation of cities. Modern technology is the last player in the co-evolution saga providing momentum to evolve. Cultural norms that have been somewhat stable are no longer working. There is a rethinking of technology's impact on humanity and how culture will shift. For example, humans were not quick to evolve to digital changes like Twitter as a medium of communication and dialogue, but the culture was. It has become a medium for hiring and firing, public policy statements, civil and uncivil debate, and an influencer of ideas. As an instant tool for interaction, it is an example of a new form of power. It is a power that questions the status quo and norms of society. It pushes back against traditional thinking and values, acting without the fear of failure. A new generation of thinkers is challenging how things were supposed to be. Instead of a trajectory of life that moved upstairs one step at a time, any fall from that direction resulted in alienation to the abyss, never to return. The new type of power understands that failure is never an endpoint. People have begun to figure out that old ways are not working in times of rapid change. To find new ways to succeed and fail must be experienced.

Just as the decision to accept change evolves thinking and changes behaviour, the decision to act without fear of failure becomes a new form of power. That power comes with a massive payoff, the ability to learn from failing. The wisdom of learning from failure is incontrovertible. Yet organisations that do it well are extraordinarily rare. This gap is not due to a lack of commitment to learning. Managers in most enterprises genuinely wanted to help their organisations learn from failures to improve future performance.

In some cases, they and their teams had devoted many hours to after-action reviews (post-mortems), but time after time, those efforts led to no real change. The reason: those managers were thinking about failure in the wrong way (Edmondson, 2011).

Many executives believe that failure is bad. They also believe that learning from it is pretty straightforward: ask people to reflect on what they did wrong and encourage them to avoid similar mistakes in the future, and assign a team to review and write a report on what happened and then distribute it throughout the organisation. These widely held beliefs are misguided. Effective learning is strategically producing failures. Researchers in basic science know that although their experiments will occasionally result in spectacular success, a large percentage of them (70% or higher in some fields) will fail. Exceptional organisations go beyond detecting and analysing failures and try to generate intelligent ones for the express purpose of learning and innovating (Edmondson, 2011).

The power to act without fear of failure is significant because everyone who has a stake in the past runs the risk of failing and seldom tries the new thing. Because they do not try the new something, they inherently make the system more fragile. The weaker the system is, the bigger the risk of more catastrophic failures. The power to fail is the power to take risks and defies conventional wisdom. It is a new form of power. Its impact on the culture is already evident and will become a more dominant part of all global cultures. Leaders who can think for themselves and think beyond the boundaries of conventional wisdom will be more welcomed in education, the corporate world, politics, and elsewhere. This indicates a shift in cultural norms that previous heroes have become losers, and a new set of heroes is emerging.

Jeff Bezos is widely known as the CEO of Amazon, currently the richest man in the world, and it's clear that his success did not just come from nowhere. He left the security of a high-level position at a Wall Street investment firm to start Amazon, which at the time of its inception was just an online bookstore. Bezos understood the risks of starting over and building a company from the ground up. He even warned his earliest investors, his parents, that there was a 70% chance Amazon would fail. Bezos has based his risks on what he calls a 'regret minimisation framework'. Instead of assessing how much risk a decision has, he instead questions if he will regret a decision in the future (Eyak, 2019).

Millionaire. Philanthropist. Genius. These are some adjectives used to describe Elon Musk, another of the new breed of risk thinkers. This entrepreneur founded the remote payment service PayPal, owns Tesla Motors (manufacturers of electric sports cars), is head of Space X (the first private firm to travel to space under contract with NASA), is the inspirer of Solar City (a company that develops technology based on photovoltaic energy) and is responsible for Halcyon Molecular (a biotechnology laboratory that seeks a cure for various diseases). Musk displays a boldly wild imagination and a high tolerance for risk (Isaacson, 2021).

Jack Ma is the founder of the e-commerce giant Alibaba and is a stakeholder at Alipay, its sister company, an e-payment portal. Before April 2021, he was the richest man in China, with an estimated net worth of $25 billion, on the back of the recent world-record $150 billion initial public offering (IPO) filing of his company. He was an English teacher, not an internet programmer and certainly not a technology pro. He was an optimistic and determined entrepreneur who changed the face of business and the Internet in China and worldwide. Being persistent in the face of adversities and treating rejections and failures was Ma's opportunity to succeed. New forms of power slowly impact society, and new cultural norms are emerging (Zitelmann, 2020).

## Core Strength

The term core strength comes from the world of athletics, muscle training, and visiting the gym. Members learn how to build muscle mass and muscle tone in the gym. It is done by working the muscles to exhaustion. It is called muscle failure, and although it sounds serious, it simply means working the muscles until they give out. The objective is to push the muscle to the point where the muscle fibres break. As they are rested, they reassemble themselves with a few more fibres than they had. The process has built more muscle. Repeated over time, the body changes as muscle mass and strength increase.

This model of purpose, practice, and perseverance has some interesting similarities to applying failure power to strengthen the potential for success. The application of purposeful thought, decisions, and practice will have the same effect on the brain as it does on the body. Every failure facilitates learning. Neurologically, the learning process in the brain is the development of neuron pathways that connect different areas. Neurons are continually sending out tendrils and connections to each other. This is how memory works and how habits and pathways are determined. When that happens, a soft white material is secreted that forms a thick sheath around axons (threads between neurons) which creates a shield called a myelin sheath that covers a neuron axon. The sheath protects the pathways and the habit. The process is called myelination. The more practice, the more neurons connect and fall under the myelin sheath, and the memories become permanent. Building new pathways and strengthening them by practice will, over time, rewire the brain. Physical muscles are built at the bodily gym and mental muscles at the failure gym.

The social and corporate cost of failure within companies is high. Today, S&P 500 companies are dropping like flies, and companies' projected longevity is decreasing. The reason for this is the more institutional memory is kept and valued, the more fragile they become and the less likely the possibility of success in the future. Leaders of these companies must aim to encourage the process of strengthening their core by strategically practising failure —not for failure's sake, but through thoughtful strategic, controlled, calculated, designed failure allowing learning to strengthen and grow the enterprise. The reason some are afraid of failure is also the same reason we were all afraid of fire. If it is not handled correctly, the house will burn down and someone could get hurt. Humans have proven their adeptness for invention by conquering the challenge of fire and are equally capable of managing the challenge of learning from failure which has become part of who we are.

The core of the mental exercise is purposely engaging in the change action without regard for the outcomes. This is not a total disregard for everything and everyone but a way of acting with the finesse that brings satisfaction and an understanding that learning is the fine edge of failure. Refined core mental strength is not just about the money or the success or the fame; it is about the journey filled with successes and failures. Leaders must understand the new road map. They must grasp the magnitude of the challenge and believe in themselves. Their core strength and mastery of the power of failure must be prioritised. They must allow themselves the luxury of failure without fear. The world is changing quickly, and the old ways of solving problems are the new problem. As the next generation of leaders begin their adventure of life, it is with hope, fervour, and encouragement that the goal is the journey and not the destination. Learning, unlearning, and relearning will move the needle to the next place.

## Bibliography

Edmondson, Amy. 2011. Strategies for Learning from Failure. *Harvard Business Review*, April. https://hbr.org/2011/04/strategies-for-learning-from-failure?registration=success

Eyal, Eran. 2019. *Jeff Bezos to Elon Musk: What True Innovators Know About Risk.* Shopin, 24 January. https://medium.com/@shopinapp/from-jeff-bezos-to-elon-musk-what-true-innovators-know-about-risk-828dfcaa17d8

Isaacson, Walter. 2021. What Makes Elon Musk Different. *New York Times*, 23 July /8 updated November. https://www.nytimes.com/2021/07/23/books/review/eric-berger-liftoff-tim-higgins-power-play.html

Psychology Tools. 2021. *Fight or Flight Response.* Psychology Tools, 30 July. https://www.psychologytools.com/resource/fight-or-flight-response/

Zitelmann, Rainer. 2020. The Jack Ma Story: Why Thinking Big Is More Important Than Technical Knowledge. *CEO Today Magazine*, 1 December. https://www.ceotodaymagazine.com/2020/12/the-jack-ma-story-why-thinking-big-is-more-important-than-technical-knowledge/

# 12

# A New Math Built on Belief

Wall Street is accustomed to companies setting and meeting expectations. All too often, companies that play this fail-safe game have begun to fail. What is going on? In the modern world, everything seems to be about numbers. It is said that data are the new oil in that data will affect economies and societies by the sheer power of data's impact. Mining the data will create tremendous value, but the numbers have changed. What has been taught in school and adopted by the analysis community is to value companies based primarily on their free cash flow, which is the cash flow that is generated from the business. The cash flow month after month is used to project it into the future. It is added up and discounted by some rate of return. That number is the company's value directly related to the free cash flow. That value is important to investors looking to purchase stock and as shareholders with an expectation of return.

The disruptive realisation is that new model companies, many of them technology-based, are entering the market with initial public offerings (IPOs) that look at the numbers differently. Many tech IPOs project no free cash flow and often prospects of not making money until some unpredictable point in the future. How can the old math compute the company valuation based on the prospect of not making money? It should be understood that this scenario is not an anomaly but normative. The cash question asked is not about free cash flow, but the rate of cash burned (expended). The better questions might be more about the plan to be conservative on its cash burn projection.

This indicates the emergence of a new kind of trust-based mathematics. The valuing of a company becomes based on the narrative presented and the story being told. It is about promises that are inferred and the motivating influence achieved. This new kind of math is starkly different from the sort of mathematics taught in business school and is still taught. This is also not the Silicon Valley pixie dust built on a wing and a prayer. It can be seen in politics, business deals, and social interaction everywhere.

*Global Business in the Age of Destruction and Distraction.* Mahesh Joshi, Gaurav Rastogi, and J.R. Klein, Oxford University Press. 
DOI: 10.1093/oso/9780192847133.003.0012

Mathematics is predictable and requires proof. A mortgage company, for example, requires proof of income history and evidence of past data to conclude that future data will be similar. This is how things work in the world. The problem with mathematics is that it assumes that the world yesterday and the day before will work the same today and tomorrow and into the future. The challenge, because of technology, is that the world is no longer working the way it has in the past. The changes in economics, politics, and business, and upheaval in society are indicators that the world is changing dramatically. Any mathematics that requires past data and draws a straight line from past data into the future is likely incorrect. The shift is perceptible everywhere, and the challenge for workers and leaders, now and in the future, is how do you plan for the future when the past no longer serves as a valid reference?

The blinding flash here is that past data are not enough to inform thinking about the future. There are too many uncertainties, unknowns, and mysteries. The rub is to figure out how to make sense of mystery and gain empowerment, clarity, and confidence to proceed into the future. The change in thinking also entails inspiring other people to think the same. Elon Musk is an example of this new math thinking. With the stated goal of changing the world of electric cars, Tesla is a public company. When analysts come in and begin asking old math questions about the rate of cash burn, how much money is needed, profit per vehicle, and how many cars will be produced, Musk stops them halfway through their questions. Why are you asking me all these boring questions? I'm going to go to YouTube and watch something interesting (Molina, 2018). You're boring me, ask me something interesting. In another part of the conversation, he paints a picture of the future where autonomous cars do not require ownership and where people will not own a car but will rely on self-driven taxis. He describes a future where autonomy requires a particular type of vehicle. This story is of a future that requires Tesla's sort of autonomy and is the company of the future. Musk was painting a picture of two interesting things: one, the old mathematical questions of precision are no longer relevant; and two, understanding the future story is the only investment that will make sense.

This new math storytelling was once relegated to the domain of crooks and crooked politicians and hucksters. The power of promise and influence is what storytelling is all about. True, numbers can tell a story; however, that story is not understandable and uninteresting to most. For example, write a book full of charts and graphs and automatically the number of people that will buy and read the book will drop. But put the same content in the hands of a storyteller like Malcolm Gladwell (Gladwell, 2021) and people will line up to buy it. People like stories that appeal to their intuition and give them clarity and confidence. Numbers, typically, do not move people. No one goes to war and is willing to subject themselves to death or kill some other human because they have a great spreadsheet. People go to war because they believe a story. They are being motivated enough to do something so drastic. That is the power of storytelling. Every human worker in the future has to learn to master, understand, and participate through stories that give purpose, clarity, and confidence. Stories provide the clarity to move into an uncertain future. They serve as guide maps and roadmaps.

## Imagine That

New thinking forces people to drive environmental change to examine the conventional way of doing business. The role of the human worker in the age of artificial intelligence, machine intelligence, and robotics is shifting dramatically. It will require a deep examination of human resources, strengths, and weaknesses to obtain peak performance of man and machine. The new math is opening minds to new possibilities. Enabling a new way of thinking about the nature of work and human contribution, whether physical, mental, emotional, or spiritual, is moving to centre stage. The whole playing field is pulling humans out of mediocrity and complacency, incentivising thinking about our unique qualities as a species. The process becomes proof of the concept. Thinking capacity, imagination, conceptualisation, and visualisation drive distinctive creativity that is not yet part of the digital framework.

One of the first skills to be mastered is that of self-discipline. Regardless of terminology, developing skills that enable the management of personal awareness and creating thought paths that drive positive action are a leader's number one challenge. Whether it is meditation, introspection, spiritual discipline, study, prayer, or philosophy, the cognitive focus and clarity create an island in disruption, creating revelatory insight. These change thinking and build habits that drive emotion, which drives behaviour. An example is the spiritual discipline of yoga. The ritual of learning the art of pranayama (or practising breathing and breath management) is a step towards managing all personal energy. It creates a mental picture of taking in a breath and exhaling. The idea of taking in the energy in the air and exhaling life translates into understanding personal energy. It connects with the ability to inspire and motivate others to action. The ability to be inspired and to inspire is distinctively human.

For millenniums people have looked at the stars and imagined shapes. The shapes were seen but were nothing more than straight lines or curved lines of stars. Imagination, however, conceptually connects the dots, and picture constellations become visible in the sky. That connecting of the dots produced the creation stories, which allowed ancient people to understand or explain the world around them.

That same capability to work in a situation with incomplete information without all the data is commonplace in an age where there are an infinite number of things to know. The job of today's leaders to connect only a few dots of data into a coherent shape is a solely human trait. Steve Jobs was skilled at telling what was happening, helping people understand the story. His stories excited and inspired people to look forward to the story's unfolding. Stories are things that motivate and move the culture forward.

The education system has struggled with preparing the most human skill of storytelling in this new environment. Many systems begin and end with a presentation of dry facts and dry data put onto charts and tables that end up being a file full of information and no capacity to understand them. Leadership's ability to connect the dots is always about thinking and projecting outside the data. Available data are always going to be limited. What needs to be taught and learned by workers and leaders is seeing things without complete information. It is the ability to see things without full details and find meaning and clarity in the story. This drives using that meaning and clarity to move forward and influence others through words and actions. These are intimately connected essential human skills that predate spoken language. The abilities to paint, tell stories, and imagine the future are still inherently human skills that remain valuable.

## Data Paralysis

Until recently, the business world has been led by old math leaders that were experts in numbers. When Walmart grows its revenue by 3%, it results from an intricately devised plan. Details are tracked down to the last number, last store, and last class inventory, following the plan results in a 3% increase in revenues. In contrast, the new math has companies like WhatsApp, which goes from zero to 600 million users in its first few quarters. This could be classified as a miracle, having been tried by many companies using the old math with the only result being failures. It was not because planning is the problem. It is not that lack of imagination is the problem.

Anyone who does not know how to dance will say it is not the right time or not the right moves or is not quite the right beat that will work. They wait for every condition to be right before jumping into the dance, and they will most likely never have the right conditions. People are paralysed by data and paralysed by the lack of data. An excessive amount of time is spent gathering the data, testing the thesis and hypothesis, and finally realising there are too much data. So much information makes sense that it is impossible. This scenario happens in corporate bureaucracies and boardrooms where safety is important and a big challenge for companies and entrepreneurs. The entrepreneur is filled with excitement and dread simultaneously.

The fundamental problem of thought is understanding the nature of knowing. Some things are known, and these can be counted and measured. Some things can be known and some things cannot be known. Recognising these three concepts can set the stage for insight and imagination or drive things down a rabbit hole. The key becomes understanding what is known and what can be known, and accepting that some things are beyond comprehension. Waiting for all the data and exhaustively sorting through and proofing every piece can easily become a never-ending process. Following that strategy results in paralyses and inaction.

Understanding and embracing the mystery of the unknowable and that adding more data is not the solution is the prescription for immobility. The conventional corporate model has always been to figure everything out and then act, because it was important to be safe and small. The entrepreneur's model is the opposite, with action coming first and then figuring it out. The nature of the world right now is entrepreneurial. The technology of machine intelligence can handle the knowables. Machines are designed to gather data, digest it, and provide the best, most efficient solutions. It is humans that must address the mystery of the unknowable.

It is the ability to embrace that mystery that sets man apart from machines. The ability to look at random dots and see a pattern or a picture is uniquely human. This imagination is embedded in the history of stories that have informed, inspired, and motivated the movement of culture. There is little present on this Earth that does not have its story. Humanity's real conquest is rooted in the stories, from ideologies to entertainment to science. As leaders begin to understand the machine and human workforce, each has a role. Everything that can be automated will be automated. It will be cheaper, more efficient, and more effective. Those things that require creativity, ingenuity, innovative energy, and imagination will still require human presence. It is about building a system of trust and belief.

## Believe It or Not

The human brain is hardwired to sort out or make sense of everything that reality presents. This neurological capacity stages the propensity for storytelling. The task is to rebuild the essential trust in the innate ability to learn and tell stories. This belief has been educated out of the human cognitive DNA through the ideological designs of the education system. Rebuilding that belief is about trusting that things can change and imagining the path. This is a voyage of discovery that consists not of seeking new landscapes but of looking with fresh eyes.

This new vision is the ability to see that the world is different and to see things that are only dots to be connected. It is the ability to live with an incomplete dataset and still act. It is something that has to be learned but must be rediscovered. It recognises the acquired habits waiting for the perfect moment to become a distraction. This does not mean giving way to superstition but constantly testing the story against new information. It is about acting on the best available data and continually testing and changing.

It also involves the practical idea of learning new skills and building habits. These are tools to help in understanding, visualising, and practising change. Tools like doodling, journaling, or creating mind maps of thinking and ideas can help organise, clarify, and remember. These types of tools will also assist in learning how to tell stories and understand the shape and trajectory of stories. It will help to understand the emotional appeal of stories and how to influence other people using that emotional appeal.

## Bibliography

Gladwell, Malcolm. 2021. *Malcolm Gladwell.* Malcolm Gladwell, 28 June. https://www.gladwellbooks.com/

Molina, Brett. 2018. Elon Musk Dismisses Talk of Tesla Cash Crunch: 'Boring Questions Are Not Cool'. *USA Today*, 3 May. https://www.usatoday.com/story/tech/talkingtech/2018/05/03/elon-musk-scolds-analysts-tesla-call-boring-questions/576484002/

# PART 4
# LEADING FORWARD

# 13

# Computers Were Once People

Throughout human history, humans have counted on the digits of their hands. When astronomers calculated the next eclipse or the arrival of a comet, the calculations were done with the heads helped by hands, log tables, and slide rules. After the Great Depression in the 1930s, the United States government created the Works Process Administration (History, 2021). A significant part of the work done by this agency involved statistics, all of which was computed by human computers. These computers went to work every morning, took lunch breaks, and had holiday parties (Garber, 2013). Computers were once people.

Domesticated beasts of burden and mechanised machinery had already taken over humans' physical tasks and drudgery, but computation requires higher skills. Humans did the jobs of adding, multiplying, projecting, and recalculating. No workhorse could do this work, and the only choice was to use humans. Humans could do complex tasks and computational wizardry required for basic commerce, warcraft, and other technological advances like the printing press or the flying buttress.

As the need for solutions became more multifaceted and complex, the human mind created machines that could do simple computations. Humans could no longer handle all the data, the computational flexibility, and the precision required for calculation. As they did before, to manage tasks more efficiently or carry out undoable tasks, non-human machines were invented to solve problems. As late as 1939, when Barbara 'Barby' Canright joined California's Jet Propulsion Laboratory as the first female 'human computer', the nomenclature indicated the idea (Holland, 2016). With the advancement of technology, humans' definition of a computer has, through time and experience, morphed into a new meaning and designation.

As digital computers move into traditional human domains, global society is being altered in two significant ways. Digitalisation's disruption destroys the old ways of working, thinking, and relating. The distraction from digitalisation is changing the way humans engage with themselves,

*Global Business in the Age of Destruction and Distraction.* Mahesh Joshi, Gaurav Rastogi, and J.R. Klein,
Oxford University Press. © Mahesh Joshi, Gaurav Rastogi, and J.R. Klein (2022).
DOI: 10.1093/oso/9780192847133.003.0013

each other, and as a collective society. Humanity's response to these two challenges will be creating a new culture.

As computers continue to become more powerful and data become plentiful and inexpensive, the prospect of artificial intelligence (AI) taking over more human characteristics is unnerving to some. Amid the explosion of technology, no place is immune from its impact. Much time and cognitive energy can be spent on the foibles of the future of digital technology, but the focus of this conversation is to consider its impact on humans.

## Man on the Mountain

The human part of the equation requires skill, craftsmanship, intellect, discernment, wisdom, nuance, and discipline. Computers cannot master these basic human characteristics, and they remain the domain of human endeavour. Ancient wisdom would approach the conundrum with enthusiasm, so this process moves forward.

The conversation begins with thinking about the 'man on the mountain', who is currently at the top of the hierarchy. These are leaders in positions of influence, wealth, and power worldwide. Today the man on the mountain is unhappy. Not many people with momentous wealth and power live on the top of the socio-economic mountain that overlooks the flat plains of everyone else. Wealth distribution inequities are starkly evident like a mountain in a vast wasteland.

For explanatory purposes, imagine that one man is on top of the mountain today. Even though this man is on the mountain with access to everything, there is still unfulfilled desire and displeasure with the current situation. The myth of modernity is that money and power are the sources of all that is good and glorious. On the flat plains, the mantra remains actual hard work, and perseverance on the ladder will lead to success. At the top of the ladder, the reward is to be the man on the mountain.

Former US Surgeon General Vivek Murthy states that 40% of Americans report feeling lonely, and the actual numbers may be even higher (Murthy, 2017). The purview is not better on the mountain, as Murthy cites another survey (Saporito, 2012) that half the CEOs reported having loneliness that affects their performance. The personal impact of being lonely is the equivalent of smoking 15 cigarettes a day. Murthy calls this the 'loneliness epidemic', which is indeed all around us.

The loneliness epidemic (Chatterjee, 2018) arrives at a time of profound changes in the outside world. The loneliness also signals a disconnection with the immediate environment, communities, and cultures. The lack of connection begins with the lack of self-awareness that alienates and distracts from feelings, thoughts, and our passions. Like the air-filled plastic bubbles that line packing boxes, people become empty outside and inside and use coping mechanisms as padding against damage.

Empty leaders cannot lead. Even from the top of the mountain, the distant path remains blurred. Impaired thinking in leadership affects confidence and impacts clarity and purpose. The first step of foundational leadership is introspection that begins to clarify the journey and provide insight into thoughtful perpetual growth.

An example of this thoughtful perpetual growth is the traditional culture of yoga. The yogis were the original knowledge workers, deeply engaged in unveiling the true nature of reality. With precise language, careful instructions, and a system of checks and balances, the yogis were scientific in their approach in ways that the modern scientist would recognise and respect. This thinking presents some principles that offer common-sense insight.

## The Discipline of Now

First, the ability to master personal time and organisation is an essential trait for a leader. Understanding the moment itself and being in the moment is a core part of a leader's spiritual practice—to not feel the 'tyranny of the clock' while making important decisions. This defines unflappable leaders. This includes the ability to handle layers of time, to tell a story with a narrative arc that draws upon history and projects into the future, and to foresee the future and forestall future happenings before they have happened, averting future trouble. All of these have to do with mastery of time as a leader.

Yogis see the concept of being present in the moment as touching a giant cosmic wheel and experiencing a moment that is here and then gone, only to be replaced by another moment. Understanding the importance of 'now' and its relevance and connection to history and the future enables a leader to manage the process of analysis and strategy. It helps clarify the value and fragility of decisions and drives the demand for critical thinking.

Leaders need to have the ability to slow down time. Most are masters at multitasking and have experienced the dismay of serial tasking, with its vast time commitment. Though multitasking can breed efficiency, it can also result in the oppression of the clock, i.e. trying to do too many things at once. The ability to slow down time is mastering the ability to focus attention and direct it wilfully to the desired subject. Pay attention or pay the price. Most people do not know how to pay attention and so end up paying the price. Some tools can help. One of the most common is to spend time in meditation or introspection. It allows the mind to stop running into many different things (multithreading) and to slow down time by focusing on one thing.

Knowing the value of time is another important concept. In his commencement address at Stanford, Steve Jobs said: 'Your time is limited, so don't waste it living someone else's life. Do not be trapped by dogma, which is living with the results of other people's thinking. Do not let the noise of others' opinions drown out your inner voice. And most importantly, have the courage to follow your heart and intuition' (Jobs, 2005). His comment about not being trapped by dogma is about valuing your own time and respecting the time of people around you, not wasting time on things that are not your natural genius, and not wasting time doing things that are not going to bear fruit.

Patanjali, a Hindu philosopher, says 'future suffering is avoidable'. People who live in Houston, for instance, know to look at the weather radar reading to see when the next big hurricane is coming. When it is seen, houses are closed, cars are fuelled up, and evacuation plans are made. In business, there can be hurricanes visible for years before making landfall. The leader's job is to prepare the company to survive a future crisis that is known and imminent. The challenge is that it is inconvenient to act today because it is likely that only the leader can see the coming storm. Others either do not see it, or do not experience it, or do not understand the urgency to act now. The Houston resident knows that the inconvenience in packing up the car and leaving is nothing compared to the discomfort of having the roof blown off. It is the same thing while running a company; the future suffering on account of today's inaction is avoidable.

Transformational leaders understand that this moment is a single moment in a sequence of infinite moments behind and beyond. They know that one cannot make up for endless time passed or change the time that is yet to come in this single moment. One can only deal with this moment. Knowing this in confidence, leaders must act now, not in haste, but with wisdom. Good leaders recognise the value of time, theirs and everybody else's, and master the art of slowing time through the process of introspection and meditation, directing attention to the things that are urgent and require attention. The paradox is that slowing down thinking creates more time because more work gets done. Finally, there is being aware of things that are going to happen in time. The man on the mountain should be able to see far into the distance. Destruction is all around, and if a leader is distracted, the destruction is invisible yet inevitable.

## The Heart Speaks Aloud Silently

The cultivation of the inner being, the heart, is an intensely spiritual practice that should be included in the learning curriculum in corporate careers. Cultivating the spiritual heart is possibly the most important thing a leader could do for themselves, their families, and their companies. When someone is a bold leader, they say they have a big heart or are courageous or fearless. When someone is a good team leader, they lead with their heart. It comes from the heart when someone delivers a great sales pitch or a great investor pitch.

In secular language, the words used most often are passion and enthusiasm. As anyone who has attended corporate earnings meeting will attest, intellectually constructed but dull presentations can be tedious. No one is inspired or roused by reading a restaurant menu filled with names and numbers. When the brain runs out of glucose, it does not have any more energy or willpower. The real source of energy is the psychic or spiritual heart. This is the heart of which the modern western world has little knowledge. Some part of the developed world lives in their heads and ideas. They live in things that are computed in their heads. However, a leader that has made a connection with an audience or connected with the thinking of others understands it is the heart that is the true source of energy. The first connection needs to be with their passion or enthusiasm for the leader. It is the source of energy, clarity, and purpose. It is the connection to the 'why' in the equation.

The connection between a leader and the audience is through the heart's passion. When people talk, they only partly pay attention to the words being used. They are paying attention to the tone and tenor of the voice, and they are paying attention to the speaker's presence, their body language, and their bending of the space-time around them. Research (Argyle et al., 1970) suggests that listeners respond more to non-verbal cues than to the intellectual content of the ideas. A leader's job is to lead people into the unknown, which requires intellectualising and the ability to connect to people's hearts and passion. It is not only through words but also through their passion that a leader finds a following.

The revelation connects the heart with the centre of everything. Neuroscientists say that conscious experience is a thin veneer and the rest of personal bodily experience is unconscious (Morse, 2006). The rest of the universe itself is consciously unavailable. The only way to connect with everything is through the heart, and that is why cultivating passion is an important spiritual practice for leaders. The language of each culture and tradition varies. Modern western societies think of this as intuition or 'knowing' extending beyond just the intellectual capability to grasp a topic.

This concept sheds some light on the US Surgeon General's report on loneliness. Leaders who are unable to connect with their passions cannot connect with others around them. Loneliness comes back in the form of lower energy, low engagement, low enthusiasm for work, low creativity, and, ultimately, low outcomes. A hard-core business leader that does not know how to connect is doing the business disservice.

## A New Kind of Math

For years, math has been taught as a dry, exact, and straightforward concept, just as leadership skills have been presented. Leaders need to learn a new kind of math, a different way of approaching the whole idea of leading. A decade or two ago, rising managers were taught to look at how much effort it takes to save 10% margin and make the product 10% more profitable. In that math version, 1+1 equals 2, which makes sense, but only in a contained context. That sort of linear math is a limiting view of the world, and it is not incorrect, but it is a small part of what is true.

The world has more examples of that kind of math. Creativity itself is about going away from the old type of math. In his famous 2007 iPhone launch, Steve Jobs showed three pictures on the screen. He said we have a new phone, a new browser, and a new music player. Then he said, we are giving you just one thing—an iPhone! It is a new kind of math, creating something that does not exist.

It might seem miraculous thinking to people, but the whole world is miraculous. The fact that something exists where there was nothing is itself creative math. The leader who is creating the future must be willing to understand and engage with the new kind of math. They must understand that the world has many opportunities rather than just limiting ways of doing anything.

## The Process of Remembering

There is a Sanskrit[1] word, *Sanskaar*, that can be translated loosely as habits, processes, or groups of habits that have been formed knowingly or unknowingly. Running a large or small company involves developing habits that are typically problem-avoidance habits. It is a process of trial and error that adopts one solution and rejects what does not work. Eventually, rules get built into institutional memory of what is unacceptable and what is acceptable. The longer a company exists, the more knowledge base garbage is carried along in processes and cultural memory.

As the world changes and offers new challenges, this accumulated learning can become a detriment. Companies and teams must be willing to form new habits and let go of old ones. Although it is comfortable doing things the way they have always been done, the long-loved processes, systems, and culture must constantly be challenged.

GE and Toyota, for example, have had tremendous success with their quality processes and culture of precision. Still, with the world changing fast, these systems bring innovation inertia that can become fatal. Today's most innovative and successful companies are Silicon Valley start-ups and not the lumbering giants of decades past. They were thought to be future-proofed with leadership thinking that the business is sound and stable and will not be affected by what is to come.

Executives from great process companies usually fail as leaders of entrepreneurial ventures. They are used to a particular process and organisational capability lacking in a start-up. Large companies did not design the process but inherited or co-built a culture. As they move to a new environment, they are completely at a loss, not knowing how to respond to the challenges of that particular time.

Learning to let go of bad habits and acquiring new habits is also important, and those are both important. This unlearning and relearning is essential for personal and corporate renewal. All this is not to suggest that

[1] An ancient Indo-European language of India, in which the Hindu scriptures and classical Indian epic poems are written and from which many northern Indian (Indic) languages are derived.

companies should replace their experienced management with inexperienced upstarts. The age or years of experience are not a helpful metric, but mental and spiritual agility is. If decades of experience come with an accumulated fear of things known and unknown, then the years of experience can be a debilitating factor. If the experience brings creative confidence and resilience, then the years are well added.

As automation and AI take on more human jobs, the resulting changes will reshape the workplace entirely. Leaders will need new skills to manage themselves and their organisations.

## Bibliography

Argyle, Michael, Veronica Salter, Hilary Nicholson, Marylin Williams, and Philip Burgess. 1970. The Communication of Inferior and Superior Attitudes by Verbal and Non-Verbal Signals. *British Journal of Social and Clinical Psychology*, Vol. 9, Issue 3:222–231

Chatterjee, Rhitu. 2018. Americans Are A Lonely Lot, and Young People Bear the Heaviest Burden. *National Public Radio*, 1 May. https://www.npr.org/sections/health-shots/2018/05/01/606588504/americans-are-a-lonely-lot-and-young-people-bear-the-heaviest-burden

Garber, Magan. 2013. Computing Power Used to Be Measured in 'Kilo-Girls'. The Atlantic, 16 October. https://www.theatlantic.com/technology/archive/2013/10/computing-power-used-to-be-measured-in-kilo-girls/280633/

History. 2021. FDR Creates the Works Progress Administration (WPA). History, 4 May. https://www.history.com/this-day-in-history/fdr-creates-the-wpa

Holland, Brynn. 2016. Human Computers: The Women of NASA. History, 13 December. https://www.history.com/news/human-computers-women-at-nasa

Jobs, Steve. 2005. 'You've Got to Find What You Love,' Jobs Says. Stanford News, 4 June. https://news.stanford.edu/2005/06/14/jobs-061505/

Morse, Gardiner. 2006. Organizational Culture, Decisions and Desire. Harvard Business Review, 1 January. https://hbr.org/2006/01/decisions-and-desire

Murthy, Vivek. 2017. Work and the Loneliness Epidemic. Harvard Business Review, 26 September. https://hbr.org/2017/09/work-and-the-loneliness-epidemic

Saporito, Thomas J. 2012. It's Time to Acknowledge CEO Loneliness: Harvard Business Review, 15 February. https://hbr.org/2012/02/its-time-to-acknowledge-ceo-lo

# 14

# Distraction Is the New Addiction

Distraction is big business. This is the Age of Distraction, and there is no end in sight. Though framed as the Information Age or the Fourth Phase of the Industrial Revolution, it is rightly the Age of Distraction. Technology-driven waves of connection and information constantly wash over almost every aspect of life. As change rides those waves, it brings opportunity, access, and creative innovation that have disrupted business, organisations, the workforce, and lifestyle. The bright side of this brave new world is that these changes have the prospect of affecting equity, climate, poverty, and global relationships that humans have struggled with for millenniums. The dark side is buried in the curious human psyche where we are prone to focus on whatever new curiosity is presented. The human mind is easily distracted. In an age where distraction is everywhere, it is having a heyday. Coupled with the innovative nature of humans, the result is a system built to use distraction to garner attention and thereby gain access to billions of minds. Distraction has been weaponised and is pervasive. It is highly corrosive to individuals, societies, economics, politics, and businesses. As the intensity of distraction continues to increase, its impact becomes more evident. It becomes highly corrosive and threatens to damage some of the basic systems and sectors that sit at the foundation of society. The process, however, is completely reversible. Humans can reverse the effects of distraction. It involves reaching back into the basics of our cognitive facilities and applying the initiative of self-discipline.

As the technological cycle of change remains prevalent, with its destructive and distractive attributes, the traditional business model is being destroyed, and a massive data overload impacts thinking. What once was the staple of strategic decision-making has become the distraction of data overload. Knowledge does not always create wisdom, and sometimes it creates confusion. These distractions impact the future of work, the workforce, and the monolithic corporate business model. Companies will use a

*Global Business in the Age of Destruction and Distraction.* Mahesh Joshi, Gaurav Rastogi, and J.R. Klein,
Oxford University Press. © Mahesh Joshi, Gaurav Rastogi, and J.R. Klein (2022).
DOI: 10.1093/oso/9780192847133.003.0014

distributed workforce shared with other companies, and workers will experience more remote working experience and learn to reinvent themselves in quick cycles.

Every age is measured by what people value. In the East India Company, which ruled India from 1757 to 1857, the industrial products were the measure of value. That remained the prominent measure for companies and became in modern times market capitalisation. Companies with solid market capitalisation were dominant for decades. It became known as the Industrial Age. In this new age, cultural valuation looks not only at market capitalisation. In 2011, of the top ten companies globally by market capitalisation, six were oil and gas or industrial companies. At the end of 2017, five of the top ten companies were technology companies that specialised in distraction. These companies have made the art of distraction a measure of value beyond comprehension. They have launched a weapon of mass distraction. Today those five companies (Apple, Google, Facebook, Amazon, and Microsoft) have a market capitalisation of over $9 trillion (Szmigiera, 2021).

## Monetisation of Distraction

The subtleties of the weaponisation of distraction are the development of systems designed to distract users. The more attention people pay, the more mind space can be occupied. People virtually rent out spaces in their minds for other companies to serve up advertisements and market products or ideas. The systems are designed to facilitate users' willing cooperation by buying things. This includes new smartphones with new social media tools and continuously checking phones dozens of times daily. The systems are to keep customers distracted.

Because of their physiology, humans have always looked for distraction. They have always been drawn to what is new or different. The challenge is that now distraction is highly addictive. It is addictive because the same kind of science that went into tobacco marketing is currently being used in an advanced form by computer algorithms that do all the hard work. Tobacco companies are in the nicotine delivery business. The addictive nature of tobacco is known and understood. Their strategy is to create ways to get people hooked on their product. They use analogue or organic methods like focus groups, test cities, and demographic propensities to figure out how to get people onto the nicotine habit. Fast-food companies used the same methodology. They spend a lot of time figuring out what colour combination, price combination, and smells should greet customers in their restaurants. They examine how much salt, fat, and sugar their food should contain and what labels encourage people to buy. This organic system is designed to distract people and get their attention to build a habit of addiction.

The same process has been upgraded to run with algorithms that never sleep or take vacations. They calculate data points and potential outcomes in milliseconds. They are now beginning to understand addictions, running tests, and learning how to make things more addictive. The distraction delivery businesses are always looking for what kind of vibration alert, blurb, or haptic touch will keep customers' attention and business. At the end of the day, the customers are complicit in giving away their attention.

## Distraction Is Pervasive

There are few places around the globe where hyperdistraction does not exist. It is unavoidable, with continuous interruptions and distractions being part of life. Social media is everywhere and growing. Facebook Messenger has more than 1.3 billion users and sends 8 billion messages daily (Review 42, 2021). WhatsApp has more than 2 billion users and handles 100 billion messages a day (Oberlo, 2021). Just these two make up a significant number, representing nearly half of the world's 7.7 billion population.

Distraction is highly pervasive if for no other reason than the number of people who have smartphones. They have access to email, text messages, Facebook, Twitter, WhatsApp, and many social media outlets. Fear of Missing Out (FOMA) is prevalent, with people constantly checking email, Twitter, or other social media feeds. Distraction occurs at every ding of the smartphone. In addition, people create their own distractions by posting messages and continually checking to see how many 'likes' have been garnered. In seeking friends, they miss out on any type of social engagement.

Many times, distractive attention is driven by fear. Human innovation has created algorithms that monitor interests and behaviour. These algorithms have discovered that people like sensational things or things that provide an undue advantage. The result is social media serves up a steady diet of fear and greed. The perception becomes that the only narrative is nothing but negative news. In reality, what is being presented is the strangest, worst-possible news that has been created around observation. It creates frenetic fear and urgency that the next disaster lurks around the corner. It is a 24/7 news cycle driven by distraction's pervasiveness. This is a system of mutually assured distraction. Though the algorithm and networks constantly distract, people are perpetuating it and are now cauterised by it. It has become commonplace. Users essentially gift their attention to somebody else and no longer have control or access to their attention.

## Distraction Is Corrosive

Distraction is corrosive not merely in terms of personal productivity but also in terms of relationships, awareness, and physical and emotional stress. Though it feels like something sweet and harmless, it is highly corrosive. Initially, it is a cause of declining personal productivity. Voluminous interruptions inhibit the ability to apply the full power of intellect, passion, and energy to internal awareness and access the deep thinking and focus that leads to salient problem-solving. Another victim is alienation from engagement with others. The loss of engagement with self, work, and society has a negative impact. In things that require continuous human attention, the processes will break down. It can be small things, like forgetting an important date, or more severe, like the train accident caused by the engineer texting at 80 miles per hour. The corrosive nature of distraction is also visible in physical and emotional stress. It is important to think about what it does physically and mentally. Harvard Business Review reported that the distraction of information workers resulted in the loss of ten points of IQ because of distraction and overload (Hemp, 2009). The loss of IQ inhibits their ability and capability to perform. It slows down processes.

When processes slow, people work longer hours dealing with information overload that they cannot handle because of distraction's corrosion of mental capacity. Information overload is about an attention shortage more than an excess of information. But it's more a story of how we are so distracted that we cannot handle the data. Research indicates that two-thirds of companies feel their employees are overwhelmed by work (Stiles, 2015). That feeling of being overwhelmed now shows up in physical and emotional stress. People are feeling disengaged with their workplace, communities, and relationships.

This is a cultural phenomenon that has disengaged people from themselves. Distraction has replaced common sense and the deep work of discipline and self-control, and it has become familiar and unnoticeable. People tend not to have an awareness of their lack of attention. As a result, the ability, capacity, and motivation to do creative or innovative work that requires attention is abandoned or at the least postponed.

## Distraction Addiction Is Reversible

Just as distraction addiction has been learned through the development of habits, the process of unwinding and creating new habits is also an obtainable objective. Being able to reverse the effects of distraction is the key to success in the future. The capacity to think about the future is bound up in learning to hold on to attention, releasing the resources needed to discipline self, expand time, and increase productivity.

Distraction is reversible through conscious awareness and practice. Just as the habits of distraction were built up over time, weaning from them will take time. The first step is to be aware of the habit. Checking the phone is almost an involuntary action, beginning with small steps of recognising the habit. Habits come with their rewards. Picking up the phone at the Pavlovian beep brings the reward of satisfying FOMO. There is a cue for each habit, just as there is a reward. The signals are essentially anything that grabs attention, like boredom, a beep, a random thought, or anything that triggers the urge to change attention immediately. The key to changing the habit is to catch it at the cue level. This enables conscious control of attention and redirection of reward. It virtually allows for the rewiring of patterns. The exact mechanisms can be used in the building of new habits. Alarms, calendar reminders, or points in a routine can serve as cues to promote action towards a reward. It is essential to recognise that new habits do not happen independently. This process requires persistent deliberate practice. The output equation is relevant here. High-quality output equals time spent on activity multiplied by the intensity of action.

Understanding the output equation and learning the secrets of deep work is essential. The idea of rewiring the brain is not just a theoretical concept to motivate or entertain. It becomes important to recognise ways of identifying why we cannot get work done. It takes knowing when attention has been drawn to a distraction and learning to pay attention to enable an energy payback that strengthens performance.

There is another thing that people need to know. Brains can be rewired. Neurologically, the learning process in the brain is the development of neuron pathways that connect different areas. Neurons are constantly sending out tendrils and connections to each other. This is how memory works and how habits and pathways are determined. When that happens, a soft white material is secreted that forms a thick sheath around axons (threads between neurons) which creates a shield called a myelin sheath that covers a neuron axon. The sheath protects the pathways and the habit. The process is called myelination. The more practice, the more neurons connect and fall under the myelin sheath, and the memories become permanent. Building new pathways and strengthening them by practice will, over time, rewire the brain.

A key to the process is consciously taking time for introspection, thought, or mediation that allows for the mental reboot necessary to clean out the distraction from the cognitive process. This meditation time should not be considered a luxury but a necessary professional skill. The process helps focus attention, hold awareness, direct attention, and reset a distracted state.

## Bibliography

Georgiev, Deyan. 2022. Incredible Facebook Messenger Statistics in 2022. Review 42, 18 January. https://review42.com/resources/facebook-messenger-statistics/

Hemp, Paul. 2009. Death by Information Overload. *Harvard Business Review*, 1 September. https://hbr.org/2009/09/death-by-information-overload

Lin, Ying. 2021. 10 WhatsApp Statistics Every Marketer Should Know in 2021. Oberlo, 11 May. https://www.oberlo.com/blog/whatsapp-statistics

Stiles, Kelin. 2015. Dilemma of an Overwhelmed Employee—Why Companies Lack in Workforce Engagement. SC Blog, 18 February. https://www.surveycrest.com/blog/why-companies-lack-workforce-engagement/

Szmigiera, M. 2021. Biggest Companies in the World by Market Capitalization 2021. Statista, 10 September. https://www.statista.com/statistics/263264/top-companies-in-the-world-by-market-capitalization/

# 15
# Control Junky or Chaos Monkey

There is little doubt that the quantum discontinuity in leadership and management styles changes dramatically when destruction and distraction are in play. To lead in the future will be radically different from the monolithic corporate models still prominent. Distributed workforces, a new form of communication, and a changing technological world make leading a corporation culture stuck in old thinking impossible. Industrial Age thinking based on generations of corporate cultural development built on a legacy of experience and specialised expertise is not well suited for an age filled with distraction and disruption. These learned practices are being destroyed not only at the periphery but also at the core. Things held to be true and unquestionable, like education and vestige of experience, are turning upside down. The unsettling nature of the disruption is felt across all spheres of life. Geopolitics, economics, business, and education are being disrupted by changes striking at the core of old standards.

Significant elements are creating a change in management and leadership style. Change-driven aspects of the evolving environments such as the rise of new media with instant communication that is bidirectional allow producers and users to interact. New ideas are creating tremendous growth. Ecosystems are experiencing new engagement models and new forms of power that demand new kinds of leadership thinking. Old paradigms and time-tested concepts are being challenged, and they are being destroyed and replaced by new thinking.

## Control Versus Chaos

Paradigm companies were designed to be command and control enterprises. They are based on mechanisms of control of the organisations, people, and ideas, and how people are trained to conform to those control mechanisms. Companies and economies designed to be command and control enterprises do not work well in an environment of hyperkinetic change and chaotic situations. In the age of transformation, control is never

*Global Business in the Age of Destruction and Distraction.* Mahesh Joshi, Gaurav Rastogi, and J.R. Klein,
Oxford University Press. © Mahesh Joshi, Gaurav Rastogi, and J.R. Klein (2022).
DOI: 10.1093/oso/9780192847133.003.0015

to be assumed. Control is only temporary and might be control over one thing and not over another. Those in leadership are evolving from being control junkies to being chaos monkeys.

There is a move from the role of a leader of an enterprise, economy, country, institution, or job entailing making sure everything was under control. The new role is not to keep the chaos out but to figure out how to thrive in it. The strong-man leadership model observable in corporations and countries is being displaced by confident leaders who have no need or desire to go through focus group testing of their messaging and are satisfied by their intuitive sense. These leaders worldwide are messaging directly to the people rather than through intermediaries. They are replacing leaders who pay no attention to professional or academic experts. Many models that worked in the old paradigm no longer work in the new. The new paradigm does not rely on being in the market doing things and apologising for failure. It learns from the experience. Any expertise that does not come from that type of experience suffers from being too little too late.

The transformation to a new paradigm is happening to leaders across the world. Strong leaders who can manipulate people emotionally, positively or negatively, are overcome by innovative and different thinking. This thinking is more intuitive and responsive. It is open to the risk of failure and not only acknowledges them but uses the experience as a learning opportunity. An example is Facebook's Mark Zuckerberg, who, when asked about a product failure, responded that he had a multitude of failures yet to go. The old control model has given way to the chaos monkey model that tries and fails, learns, unlearns, and relearns.

## Change on One Hand

These demands for a different leadership style are driven by the extraordinary changes in the age of transformation. The conversation of change can be complex and confusing but can be more palatably managed using a meme. Five things can summarise the transformational nature of change, and to remember these ideas, the human hand will be the meme.

### Thumb

The first thing to be examined is the rise of new media represented by the thumb. The rise of a new kind of media and the decline in the power of old media has subtly expanded into the public consciousness. The long-accepted methods of getting information like television, newspapers, and magazines have disappeared and been replaced by connecting directly to the source. This direct connection exists in corporations, educational systems, and economies. Management of information no longer happens in some backroom but in the field and with people. The opposable thumb is what separates man from all animals except most monkeys. Being aware of the rise of new media must be followed with the mastery of new skills. The opposable thumb allows humans to hold things and grasp new things, and that ability allows us to behave differently.

This new social media, the internet, and smartphones have enabled direct access to communications. Previously, if the CEO wanted to send a message, most listeners would receive the message by reading a newspaper, book, or article, or seeing it on television. It was a system that was not direct but relied on somebody else's interpretation or editorial comment on the message. The listener usually would listen to the point of view and not directly to the CEO. Today the media is being disintermediated. The opinion-makers are not as relevant as they used to be, and Twitter and Facebook, which are also shaping opinion, are far more direct.

There is a value in direct engagement at the scale leaders can have. The capacity to talk directly and have an immediate conversation across the entire organisation can have enumerable benefits. The flip side of that type of engagement is its potential to distract and feed misinforming erroneous information. This potential requires consumer mastery of new media, and that requires self-mastery. It increases sensitivity to being overly swayed by distractive voices and helps to focus attention on other voices.

The mastery will help recognise that what is urgent is not necessarily important. New media like WhatsApp, Twitter, Facebook, and TikTok represent what is urgent because that is the nature of the medium. In real life, most messaging is not pressing, and developing the skill to avoid the pattern trap and make good decisions that prioritise behaviour is crucial. This escape from chaos adds stability, reason, and rationality to leadership character.

## Pointer

The second element is the entrance of a new playbook. Just as the pointing finger is sometimes used to indicate command or control, it also serves as a reminder that the core of the command and control economy with the language of the old Industrial Revolution is coming to its last page. The view of management as a conveyor belt where performance moves along a continuum from skill to skill and people are told exactly what to do is no longer relevant. The pointing finger of management has stopped working as companies realise that overspecialisation leads to fragility. If people only know what they are told to do when the environment changes, there is a pause to figure out what comes next.

In the 1980s and 1990s, there was a culture of 'the company way'. Companies captured the culture in documents like the Toyota way, the McKinsey way, the H.P. way, the Xerox way, or numerous other playbooks. These pieces were generally written by public relations people and were serious books written by serious academics. They delineated the company way of doing things and were the reason for success. They were successful because the world was not changing that fast. As the company culture learned to do something, it was documented and taught to an entire generation of managers. It was the one path to success internally for any rise from the bottom of the pyramid to the top through the company playbook. In that playbook, the employee could learn the way, master the way, and then direct other people to follow the course—all in one career journey that used to work just fine.

The issue that has become prominent is not that the playbooks were not followed but that they no longer work. They were designed for a world that changed slowly, and they were designed for a world where consistency and uniformity in looks and thinking were valued. These values are no longer valued in today's world of constant multidirectional change.

Understanding the direct nature and language of change cannot have people who look and think alike. The urgent demand is to be quickly absorbed and understand situations. This values having input from a diversity of opinions, experiences, and styles. The old playbooks, the old math, the old language of the Industrial Revolution, of doing the same things at scale, along the lines of a conveyor belt, and the associated style of thinking no longer work.

## Middle

The third piece that summarises the transformational nature of change is the sign of new power and new forms of power. Just as the middle finger in modern cultures is a sign of pushback and resistance, the third sign represents an incredible change in thinking. It is a change that validates the ability to fail, in contrast to the prevailing norms of society. The new form of power entails the willingness to fail, the desire to try new things and fail. Amazon's Jeff Bezos defied critics with the statement that he would try things and was going to fail. The strategy succeeded in creating numerous $10 billion businesses inside of a nearly $1 trillion company. . This is the emergence of a new form of power.

Challenging the old form of power is the personal willingness to take risks and to fail. It is the power to fail. The power to learn from failure, bounce back up, and do something else is extremely important in the chaos monkey phase of the world. Chaos permeates the world as things change quickly and then change again. The old playbook said to expect to succeed and to hide from failure. The power of failure understands that failure happens and is not the end of the world. The power is to learn the lesson, do the next things, build a new intuition, try again, event after event, and expect to fail again. This thinking is possible because technology changes the playing field by limiting the cost of failure, psychic and emotional, eliminating barriers for trying something else.

This is a new kind of power. This new form of power has not been tried in Industrial Revolution thinking. The new thinking is willing to venture into the unknown, try new things, and fail. The difference is the recognition that failure is not personal. It is also worth mentioning that the old playbook was adopted, not mandated. Asymmetric thinkers have always been the bright spots of history. Thomas Edison was one of the mad rush to invent the light bulb along with quite a few other inventors. He tried one type of filament, but it failed. He tried another kind of vacuum, but it failed. He tried another kind of glass, but it failed. When asked about his failure, he replied, 'I have not failed. I've just found 10,000 ways that won't work.' The epitome of life's failures are people who did not realise how close they were to success when they gave up.

Every failure provides new data, and every failure is a way of improving and trying something else. The only reason the market gets successful products is enough failures have been observed before discovering what works. The willingness to engage with failure positively allows success in a big way. This is a new form of power in leaders and everyone.

## Ring

Next is the ring finger, which is commonly connected to engagement. It is symbolic of developing new forms of engagement, whether users, voters, students, or leaders. Examples of these new forms of engagement are the Khan Academy and massive open online courses (MOOCs) in education, and Trump in the United States and Narendra Modi in India speaking directly to people. In chapter 3, the impact of hyphen-tech is discussed as another instance of new engagement methods. Changes in finance, hotels, health, and transportation are further examples. Uber did not invent taxis, launch spaceships or satellites, or create credit cards. They did not make any of these things, but they created a new way of engaging with drivers and passengers.

Engagement is more than just being familiar. It is about a committed relationship with consumers, users, voters, and employees and a fresh and exciting way to engage people. It is a new technique that is more endearing and satisfying to all parties. It seeks sympathetic insight into another's thinking, and it offers experiences that enable sensitivity, clarity, commonality, and simplicity.

Technology today constantly changes engagement. A customer can take a photo of a cheque and upload it to their bank account with a smartphone. That change in engagement makes the process simpler and begins to change the customer's overall perception of the bank. In some countries, there was a time when the bureaucratic mindset with its checks and balances made for a poor user interface. Consumers have learned to expect more straightforward and more intuitive experiences. Whether it is governments, educational institutions, companies, or start-ups, the key is to figure out new ways of engagement. They must be intuitively designed, with seamless digital experiences and smarter data uses.

## Pinkie

The final transformational nature of change is the factor of trust. In many cultures, the pinkie finger is a meme for making and keeping promises. This component is about understanding, cultivating belief and trust in a new kind of mathematics. In the old mathematics, if 2% of 100% is saved, 98% remains. This works well linearly, but the new kind of math is not linear. The new math has everything to do with changes and is non-linear. It calculates the non-linear component of the equation and understands that if the 2% saved is invested shrewdly, the remainder may end up being 102%.

It is understanding a new kind of math that differs from the conventional math of saving and projections, which have been used in politics and economics, and recognising that it is not enough. The new kind of math is non-linear and recognises the existence of new and different effects that have changed how the world works. For example, a new start-up taking a new idea to market does not think of linear effects, i.e. make the product, move it to the market, and sell it. Pinkie thinking is non-linear. It thinks about second-order effects like the impact on the market culture, or third-order effects like what needs to happen in the market that will help control costs and increase demand.

At its essence, it is about learning to understand and engage people in new ways that can create outsized outcomes and not just routine outcomes. If people are engaged and enthusiastic about your product, they will tell other people, thereby expanding demand. It is not about the old math of how many people, how many resources, or how many barrels of oil are being pulled out of the Earth. The new math is about how many people can be touched. How can they be engaged and made more enthusiastic about the product?

The new math is observable in politics right now. Unfortunately, it may be more outrageous math, but, nonetheless, it is an example of how to reach more people, cultivate belief, and drive change by telling people where you are going. For example, US President John F. Kennedy said that we would put a man on the moon by the end of the decade. It was a precise target, and that target seeded in people's imagination ended up with a man on the moon. That statement created a distinctly clear belief in the leader and his audience. That is an important part of a leader's job. The ability to cultivate belief in others begins with the ability created internally and externally. Leaders' ability to cultivate their own beliefs and the belief of others in a future that has not yet come is a new kind of skill for most people. It does not need to be a dynamic predictable leadership style because the momentum of society leaders has to pay attention to what is happening to move people along that direction.

In cultivating belief and a new kind of math, people want proof. They want to trust. Trying to get people to do new things is difficult because there is no proof. The phenomenon of getting people to buy into a concept without proof is the ability to cultivate belief. The power of a leader to influence consumer capacity to imagine a future that they cannot yet see is a prime number of the new math.

# 16
# Leading with Spiritual Energy

The concentration of this conversation about leading and living in the age of constant destruction and distraction has dedicated attention to the kind of changes being faced every day. It has been contemplated how the man on the mountain leadership structure has resulted in extremely unhappy leaders and disengagement being a standard piece of the workplace. The examination of the high cost of distraction represents ever-present destruction. In every sphere of life, politics, economics, and education, understanding common knowledge and those accepted and adopted standards taught by education and experience is no longer valid. Distraction mediated by technology and evidenced by the entry of new industries has signalled the destruction of the nature of industries and knowledge. Centuries of the old industrial education system creating uniform actors, action, and behaviour once considered the gold standard are no longer a virtue. The exponential rise and increase in ever-changing technology lead primarily to recalibrating the relationship between humans, technology, and culture.

This thoughtful conversation logic leads to the next pressing question. What strategies, skills, and conclusive solutions will lead to validity, relevance, and satisfaction in such an environment? The question requires new, more insightful thinking. This is a new way of engaging end-users, partners, voters, constituents, and yourself. At one time, new technologies provided society thousands of years to respond and evolve a suitable culture. The problem is that the pace has continued to accelerate from not a thousand years, a hundred years, or even ten years. Today's culture has barely a year to respond to new technology. The degree of shifting culture is hard to fathom. Technology is continuing to evolve with its own momentum.

The groundwork laid in previous chapters begins with a conversation of personal aligning of physical and emotional capabilities. Peter Drucker invented the term knowledge workers (Drucker, 1996) to describe workers whose principal capital is information. These are the programmers, physicians, pharmacists, architects, engineers, scientists, design thinkers, public

*Global Business in the Age of Destruction and Distraction.* Mahesh Joshi, Gaurav Rastogi, and J.R. Klein, Oxford University Press. 
DOI: 10.1093/oso/9780192847133.003.0016

accountants, lawyers, editors, and academics whose jobs are to 'think for a living' (Davenport, 2005).

Though a relatively recent nomenclature, the concept of workers whose main stock in trade is information is ancient. The main sources of examples of early knowledge workers are religious knowledge traditions. The two oldest world religions, Hinduism and Judaism, have traditions and individuals that were for millenniums mainly dedicated to knowledge and information. The Levites and Cohens of Judaism and the yogis of Hinduism were the original knowledge workers. These traditions have been dedicated to investigating trustworthy knowledge and individual awareness. It is worth paying attention to the concepts and philosophies that are both timeless and relevant in learning to cope with the environment to gain clarity and insight. Both are more than wearing funny hats and learning pretzel poses and are surprisingly relevant in today's world.

The conversation begins with why anyone should care. At the risk of being redundant, anyone paying attention to the current narrative about the destruction that can be seen everywhere will see that it is not slowing down. It is speeding up. The constant distraction that vies for attention is weaponised with the rise of fake news and algorithms designed to facilitate addiction. What is known and accepted is being destroyed. Incessant distractions are compromising the capability for self-knowledge, organisational knowledge, and world knowledge. The speed of change in technology and the fact that it has its own momentum means that there is no stopping the juggernaut. As it gains momentum, even those previously considered human domains are changing. Agriculture, once a primary human realm, is now heavily mechanised. Once thought a mainstay of human territory, manufacturing is almost entirely mechanised. No matter what, job description algorithms with the same name will soon appear.

The old strategy of climbing up and climbing out has reached its peak. The degree of self-knowledge and self-discipline required to keep climbing up to a point where technology cannot get to is difficult, if not impossible. The degree of discipline and expertise required for people to stay relevant is no longer present. Most people simply do not have that discipline nor the knowledge to learn the discipline. This is a sure formula for mass unemployment, disengagement, and unhappiness. It has become the most significant challenge to society. The human animal requires a rich and challenging environment to be fully engaged. The panacea of work will suffer as work begins to disappear. Man will seek alternative sources of engagement. Imagination wonders what the impact will be on society when members of the intelligent human species are given no challenges, have nothing to aspire to, or are not driven by engagement. One view sees only doom and gloom, but the flipside remembers man's resilient, innovative, intuitive, and imaginative nature and sees this as yet another fork in the road.

Until computers start asking about the meaning of the universe, such issues are the sole domain of humans. The answer is not to hide in a cave and commiserate at this fork in the road. The answer is far more rich and engaging, with the potential of a better and deeper satisfaction than ever before. It has everything to do with the nature of work changing from physical and intellectual to spiritual.

## Realignment

The need to recalibrate thinking from a physical or intellectual function to a spiritual process is a conversation worth having. 'A beginning is the time for taking the most delicate care that the balances are correct' (Herbert, 1965). Any discussion of spirituality comes with the danger of disintegrating into a territorial battle. For the sake of this dialogue, it will be defined as the quality of being concerned with the human spirit or soul rather than material or physical things. The difference between religion and spirituality is that religion is a specific set of organised beliefs and practices, usually shared by a community or group. Spirituality is more an individual practice and has to do with having a sense of peace and purpose (ReachOut.com, 2021).

The spiritual nature of the change in thinking is the same type of thinking at the root of levitical and yoga practice. Both are generally misunderstood but still used and practised. Anyone with an automobile understands the value of periodic adjustment or alignment of the wheels. Though it is not a major piece of the vehicle's operation, it can make the car's operation much better. An out-of-balance wheel causes a wobble, noise, and undue wear on the tire. With properly aligned wheels, the ride is much smoother, with less vibration and noise. In Hindi, the word *yoga* is derived from the root meaning to join or to yoke. The yoke connects to the axle, which makes the alignment metaphor more poignant. Yogis teach that the physical body, the energy body, the mental body, and the *nephesh* or self (Hebrew) are directly connected to society and the true source of the self. Yogis built a highly sophisticated system and practices, language, and culture of actual alignment or centring personal perspective. Its practice focuses on responsibility, interpersonal relationships, and individual disciplines. They provide a holistic approach that begins with posture, breathing, and body energy and extends to and beyond the mind.

These philosophies developed early, because both came from a sense of community driven by an introspective view of self. Indian and Chinese economies of 3000 years ago were strong and the people were wealthy enough to afford not to work 24 hours a day. This resulted in sitting quietly and pondering the weighty questions of life, time, and everything. This time off from work moves men and women from solely subsistence thinking to more deep thinking. Society could afford it, and it benefited from it. Cultures like these are wealthy not merely in material wealth but also in community and spiritual wealth. Western society is in much the same condition today. Though the nature of distraction is different, the pressure of life remains the same. The search is still for engagement and satisfaction. Unless people can find ways to engage more meaningfully, the inevitable will become societal chaos.

These early spiritual philosophies and later entries, i.e. Buddhism, Islam, and Christianity, all carry spiritual traditions that are interested in the afterlife and the inward journey that unfolds moment by moment. The yogis call it relating more deeply. A commonly heard narrative is about coping with this world by running away from society. Inevitability is a flawed construct, and human history has exhibited that fact repeatedly. The divine revelation is that the choice is up to each individual, and the option is to live outwardly normal lives that are purposefully more engaged and more satisfying.

## Practicum

Conceptual thinking, while stimulating, does not always result in a course of action that leads to the next step. The pragmatic piece of any conversation begins with a commitment to primary actions. The staging of any subsequent step must be based on the choice to practise inner and outer discipline. This choice is a conscious adjustment of thinking and habit-building that increase sensitivity. These are simple things like being more aware of external surroundings and internal recognition.

It begins by withdrawing sensitive attention from the outside world and resting it on another focus like an object or a thought. Sensitive withdrawal and focus attention are the typical definitions of meditation or mindfulness. The shared tradition of these habits is the theme of relevance, respect, and value towards self and society. It is the *halacha* or 'way' in Judaism and the yoga of living deeply. Surviving in the future is about aligning mental, physical, emotional, and spiritual energies. The old math corporate ladders have too many missing steps. The distraction of lost habits and the lack of self and interpersonal engagement have led to the inability to hold focused attention and destroyed the habits of discipline. It is a spiritual discipline that can rebuild habits and allow the rhythm and routine of structure back in consciousness. It will enable the return of the ability to hold attention despite external and internal distractions.

Remember that the leaders' job is to find meaning and to find energy within themselves to excite and influence people and drive momentum. Drucker's explanation of a manager versus a leader frames managers as telling people what to do and leaders as leading people to do what needs to be done. This involves the idea of leadership energy. Culture after culture has come to the same conclusion. There is something beneath the surface of good leaders that moves, animates, and excites others. It is more than just what is said. The rule states that 7% of meaning is communicated through the spoken word, 38% through tone of voice, and 55% through body language. It was developed by psychology professor Albert Mehrabian at the University of California, Los Angeles, who laid out the concept in his book *Silent Messages* (Mehrabian, 1971). This means 93% of communication is 'non-verbal' in nature.

During a conversation, changes in vocal tone are also a noticeable non-verbal cue that contributes to your understanding of the person speaking. It can be vocal tone or speaking style; pitch, rate, and volume contribute to understanding the speaker. It might be fidgeting like shaking, biting fingernails, and playing with a pen that someone else notices. This may express to the speaker boredom, nervousness, or disinterest. Facial expressions are another non-verbal cue. Since facial expressions are closely tied to our emotions, they reveal what we think and are perhaps the most prominent non-verbal communicators in everyday life. Head movements are especially rich conveyors of communication and one of the most straightforward non-verbal cues to understand. Certain head movements tend to be culture-specific, such as nodding in agreement within western cultures.

Hand gestures punctuate the spoken word and offer valuable context about the speaker and what they are saying.

Sometimes hand gestures give clues to the speaker's emotional state. Trembling hands could mean the person is anxious or lying. Animated, grand hand gestures could indicate the person is excited or passionate about what they are discussing. Body posture can be used to determine a participant's degree of attention or involvement during a conversation. Bad posture, like slouching, may indicate the listener is bored or uninterested in the conversation.

In contrast, if the person you're speaking to is standing or sitting still and upright and leaning forward, they are signalling that they are focused, attentive, and engaged in the conversation. The physical distance between people can set the tone for the conversation. An employee who comes exceptionally close to the speaker may indicate they have something confidential to say. Other times, getting extraordinarily close or touching someone could be considered intrusive or even hostile (Smith, 2020).

Leaders who are sensitive to mastering these skills exude charisma or an energy body that people can sense. It is present when entering a room, and it is not heard and is not seen but is preserved as a presence. A presence precedes that entry into the room. This energy of presence comes from cultivating the discipline of yoga, halacha, or mindfulness and creates a gravity that attracts people. As the discipline of the personal leadership journey is mastered, it makes things easier and enables higher performance.

## Bibliography

Davenport, Thomas. 2005. Thinking for a Living: How to Get Better Performance and Results from Knowledge Workers. Boston: Harvard Business School Press

Drucker, Peter. 1996. Landmarks of Tomorrow: A Report on the New Post Modern World. Abingdon: Routledge

Herbert, Frank. 1965. Dune. New York: Ace Books

Mehrabian, Albert. 1971. Silent Messages. Los Angeles: University of California

ReachOut.com. 2021. What Is Spirituality? ReachOut.com, 29 June. https://www.ideas.org.au/uploads/resources/550/what%20is%20spirituality.pdf

Smith, Dustin. 2020. Nonverbal Communication: How Body Language & Nonverbal Cues Are Key. Lifesize, 18 February. https://www.lifesize.com/en/blog/speaking-without-words/

# PART 5

# THE FUTURE

# 17

# Leadership in an Age of Destruction and Distraction

Digital overload may be the defining problem of today's workplace. All day and night, on desktops, laptops, tablets, and smartphones, we are bombarded with so many messages and alerts that it is nearly impossible even when we want to focus. And when we are tempted to procrastinate, diversions are only a click away. This culture of constant connection takes a toll both professionally and personally. We waste time, attention, and energy on relatively unimportant information and interactions, staying busy but producing little value (Rosen and Samuel, 2015).

The old world is being destroyed. Whether in politics, technology, business, or economics, distraction poses a significant threat to performance and productivity. Distracted by constant change, the frantic cycles and weaponisation of the technologies of mass distraction are constantly vying for attention. Discussions of the quantum speed of change in lifestyle, business, and environment are widespread. The world's new technological innovations and business models attract existing legacy business players from Buffalo to Beijing. These legacy businesses were not weak, they were strong, and there was little thought that anything could change; however, as big change entered the world, those who did not pay attention paid the price. If vigilance was not a common trait and no one was watching, when the disruption came, the ramifications were inevitable. The amount of data is enormous in the current environment, and the intensity of destruction and distraction is still prevalent.

The impact is not just relegated to the organisational sphere but is even more prominent in workers and leaders alike in the workforce. Focusing on the right things is vital—from overcoming anxiety and depression disorders to learning new skills or accomplishing life goals. Our ability to focus is like a muscle: exercise it properly and its strength will grow; abuse it and it will wither. One of the biggest culprits in diminishing our ability

*Global Business in the Age of Destruction and Distraction.* Mahesh Joshi, Gaurav Rastogi, and J.R. Klein,
Oxford University Press. 
DOI: 10.1093/oso/9780192847133.003.0017

to focus is the excessive use of modern technologies, specifically smartphones, the internet, and social media (Gazzaley and Rosen, 2016). The distraction and interruption are not the most harmful impact of technological interference. Rather the continued stream of interference flowing from modern technologies impacts the quality of our performance while at the same time weakening our mental faculties required for sustained focus. This dramatic decline in performance, which arises from increased interference levels, results from the brain's inability to multitask. Contrary to popular belief, humans cannot parallel-process information for multiple tasks, which require top-down cognitive control (Gazzaley and Rosen, 2016).

Office distractions eat up an average of two hours a day per person, and that's in addition to the way people distract themselves. Human beings switch activities every three minutes, meaning they change focus up to twenty times each hour. This means that if someone applies themselves, they focus on a task for an average of eleven minutes before getting distracted, and it then takes twenty-five minutes to return to the task. Overall, distraction and wasted effort cost organisations around $650 billion each year (Monroe, 2021).

It is important to understand that human attention is a valuable, productive, and fragile resource and to find ways to protect it rather than interrupt and undermine it. In particular, it is important to evaluate so-called supportive technology that may demand more continual attention from employees than is beneficial for them or prevents them from focusing on priorities. As an understanding of mental health has evolved, it is recognised that the topic applies to much more than the most severe conditions. Indeed, like every other aspect of health, mental illness comes in different degrees for each individual it affects. The challenge for leaders is to learn how to combat mental health issues that can become chronic or contagious at work, ultimately threatening the company's strength in the same way that dry rot threatens the stability of a house (Steinhorst, 2021).

The man on the mountain entails the concept of working hard, climbing the corporate ladder to the top, and being at the top. There is some validity in that idea when the land around the mountain was stable. In a changing world, with experience comes the realisation that the ladder is unending. Leaders need to learn to be flexible and adapt, or the time at the top will be extremely dissatisfying, with a sense of disconnection with themselves and increasing loss of personal direction and an inability to lead others. The leader on the mountain is prominent in every sector, which is the problem at the top of the mountain. Many of these top leaders are broken.

Fifty per cent of CEOs feel lonely. The title is often viewed as the pinnacle of business success. With their power, influence, authority, and big paychecks, CEO positions can offer the highest stature in the business community. According to numerous studies, half of the CEOs reported feelings of loneliness in their roles, and the majority of these CEOs believe these feelings impact their performance (Carreau, 2017).

The challenge is especially paradoxical in the digital world, where CEOs are more visible than ever yet have fewer personal interactions. They are suddenly more noticeable and evident in the organisation, in the community, and often in the media. Many leaders have thousands of social media followers but do not know who their real friends are. They worry their personal interactions have far less to do with genuine friendship and trust than career ambition. It's also a natural phenomenon for employees, even senior executives, to hold back opinions and information that they fear might harm their career or others' perceptions of them (Carreau, 2017). The CEO must now appear confident and unwavering, even invincible; hence very few are comfortable showing any vulnerability. Ironically, many leaders, especially women, will admit privately to suffering from imposter syndrome and fear that they will be discovered to be incompetent (Carreau, 2017).

Although it may be tough to sympathise with a CEO who is experiencing loneliness, the simple fact is that CEO loneliness and isolation are bad for a business and all the people working there. A CEO working in isolation cannot be effective long term, and it is demoralising to their teams. Good decision-making comes from multiple perspectives and data points. In isolation, it is virtually impossible to have this. Executive loneliness does not have to be an inevitable part of the CEO's job. In fact, in today's hypercompetitive world, they cannot afford to risk isolation. Loneliness and isolation compromise their ability to make good decisions and lead the organisation forward (Carreau, 2017).

## Leader Primer

The first challenge for leaders on the mountain will be natural for some and agonising for others. They must be able to acknowledge their vulnerability and change their habits. Isolation often manifests itself in how a leader works, and simply changing some lifestyle habits can help them breathe easier and feel less intense. It involves being realistic about themselves and what they can achieve. That introspect will also help to define when to reach out for support.

Building habits is about the positive effect on the working lifestyle of small changes. What often matters most is understanding that negative feelings and a sense of isolation are not unique. The challenges and trials of leaders are quite common to all leaders and high achievers, even if some will not admit to it. The process of finding support becomes a mere matter of willpower. Looking for like-minded peers who understand the challenges and recognise the journey can provide support and a sense of confirmation or correction of the validity of strategy and implementation. Building a network of mutual support is a powerful tool.

Specific introspective tools can push leaders towards better performance and efficiencies. One is a leader's ability to handle time as an asset rather than a liability. This is an important trait for leaders and one that evades conscious identity by many. It begins with an awareness of time itself, understanding what is happening now, and living in the moment. It involves the ability to handle layers of time and not feel the tyranny of the clock. This recognition of the moment fits into the flow of history, and an unknown future. It helps us to understand the connection, which helps delineate how the current moment is spent and connected to the past and future. Awareness of the moment enables the ability to create scenarios for the future. This ability to see into the future, forestall adverse events, and obtain favourable outcomes is an essential role of leaders.

Another vital tool is the ability to slow time. This idea goes back to humans' misconception of their ability to multitask. It turns out that trying to do many things simultaneously results in an obvious perception of not having enough time. Trying to make a collective list of things takes more time than each task separately and leads to a feeling of being oppressed by the clock. The way to retrieve or regain some semblance of control is to slow time. This is the ability to hold attention and direct it wilfully to one topic at a time. Learning how to 'stop your mind' from wandering away has the effect of slowing down time and facilitating focus on one thing at a time. As the distractions are culled, the time to complete tasks expands.

Understanding the value of time as a tool is essential for leaders. This is about leaders valuing their time and valuing people's time. It involves not wasting time on things not part of the natural genre. Not wasting time and doing things that are not bearing fruit is not just common sense, it is practical wisdom. The capacity, ability, and courage to take action today can avert future suffering. However inconvenient it might be, it is worth doing it now. Mastery of time is the ability to know where you are, foresee future problems, and act.

Because the leader on the mountain can see farther and look harder at future problems, the impacts of distraction and disruption are mitigated. Distracted leaders cannot see the disruption, and they keep looking back at history and, as such, will become history.

## Discovering Passion

The primary behavioural equation says that all behaviour is driven by emotion and all emotion is driven by thought. For leaders, this somewhat pedestrian axiom is worth exploration and examination. The equation sets the foundation for one of the most critical aspects of leadership character. This is not being a character but having character. Being a person of character is cultivating those traits that are commonly accepted by society and embedded in human psychology as being important. It is captured in language as being bold, courageous, or fearless, or having a big heart. It is possibly the most important thing a leader could do for themselves, their families, and their companies. It can be expressed as passion, enthusiasm, or kind-heartedness, but regardless of the terminology, it is the one sure thing that can make a good leader a great leader.

People live in ideas. They live in things that can be computed and figured out in the brain. The brain, however, is a low source of energy, and when it runs out of glucose it begins to lose its depth and focus. The real source of energy for humans is passion. This cognitive companion is where the true source of energy lies. Leaders can connect to passion as a source not only of energy but also of clarity and purpose. It is what drives them forward and forges connections with people around them. It is the passion that attracts attention to and tantalises curiosity of not just the words being used but also how the words are spoken. People become drawn to the leader's presence even more than the philosophical ideas. Leaders connected to their hearts have the innate ability to connect to other people's hearts. That is the next thing you need to do with the heart.

Just as the heart is the centre of everything the physical body offers, so is passion the centre of existence. Some would say that conscious experience is a thin veneer, and the rest of existence is wrapped around passion. Will Roger, the American stage and film actor, vaudeville performer, cowboy, and humourist, quipped, 'If you want to be successful, it's just this simple. Know what you are doing. Love what you are doing. And believe in what you are doing' (BrainyQuote, 2021). Knowing is not about just intellectual understanding; it is about understanding oneself and exhibiting the character of passion. Love is about passion, and belief is about passion.

This passion also involves a new way of looking at things, a sort of new math. Just as old math framed concepts in the form of numbers and equations that carried concepts, a new kind of math has to be learned. The new math adds a passion that nuances those concepts with items that add other types of consideration that impact value. It creates something where nothing exists. It takes concepts that are seemingly disconnected and creates something new. When Apple presented the iPhone, incorporating the technologies of a phone, a browser, and a music player, it created something that did not exist before. In an age where data are in excess supply, there are a ton of data with no ability to connect those data points and create something new. New math looks at it from another position. It does not revert to habits or processes that have become the common wisdom. It does not go to those habits that are typically problem-avoidance types of practices. It does not revert to ideas lodged in institutional memory that have become patterns of habit, organisational thinking, or the garbage of history. The new approach is to engage old rules of convention and form new habits. Practices and processes are essential, but learning to let go of bad habits and acquiring new habits are also important. Sticking to the mantra of 'this is how we do things' is a sure-fire recipe for success when nothing is changing. When everything is changing, it is a sure-fire recipe for driving off the cliff.

## Bibliography

BrainyQuote. 2021. Will Rogers Quotes. BrainyQuote.com, BrainyMedia Inc., 20 January. https://www.brainyquote.com/quotes/will_rogers_393804

Carreau, Debby. 2017. Conquering Loneliness at the Top. Entrepreneur, 12 September. https://www.entrepreneur.com/article/294106

Gazzaley, Adam and Larry Rosen. 2016. The Distracted Mind: Ancient Brains in a High-Tech World. Cambridge, MA: The MIT Press

Monroe, Debora. 2021. This Is your Brain on Technology: The Distraction Epidemic. Informa, HDI, 26 July. https://www.thinkhdi.com/library/supportworld/2014/distraction-epidemic.aspx

Rosen, Larry and Alexandra Samuel. 2015. Conquering Digital Distraction. Harvard Business Review, 1 June. https://hbr.org/2015/06/conquering-digital-distraction

Steinhorst, Curt. 2021. A Leader's List of Mental Health Concerns at Work. Forbes, 27 May. https://www.forbes.com/sites/curtsteinhorst/2021/05/27/a-leaders-list-of-mental-health-concerns-at-work/?sh=1d7c64981915

# 18
# Balladeers and Thinkers

Conversations regarding disruption and distraction and aspects of a leader's capacity to be a flexible, risk-taking, chaos curator present a framework for change and challenge. Everyone must recalibrate their thinking to adapt to the demands of a world that seems to change daily. Dialogues about reinvention, continuous learning, controlled failure, personal introspection, and spirituality are only a few of the strategies needed to stay relevant as the future unfolds. Another tool that may seem old-fashioned today is storytelling. The best evidence from archaeology and anthropology suggests the human mind evolved with storytelling. About a million years ago, hominid ancestors began gaining control of the use of fire. It seems to have had a profound impact on their development. It provided warmth, defence against predators, and the ability to cook food—the latter with its remarkable consequences for the growth of our brains. But it brought humans something else. The fire created a new magnet for social bonding and drew people together after dark. In many cultures, one form of fireside interaction became prevalent: storytelling (Anderson, 2017). Believe it or not, leaders have been using storytelling as a handy tool for leading others since the beginning of time. Tribal leaders use stories to gain loyalty and legitimise their reign. The elders use stories to help the group make sense of the unknown, strengthen people's group identities, and record histories. Religion leaders use stories to express their beliefs and educate followers. Military leaders use stories to reduce fear and boost morale (Li, 2020).

Though storytelling may seem outdated, that is precisely what makes it so powerful. Life happens in narratives. It is how humans communicate with one another. A story can go where quantitative analysis is denied admission. It can connect with emotion, memory, understanding, and the human heart. Data can persuade people, but data do not inspire them to act. It is narrative or storytelling that fires imagination and vision and stirs the soul. Professor Jennifer Aaker from Stanford University found that only 5% of students remembered a statistic but 63% remembered a story (Aaker and Smith, 2010). Storytelling communicates values, complex organisation

*Global Business in the Age of Destruction and Distraction.* Mahesh Joshi, Gaurav Rastogi, and J.R. Klein,
Oxford University Press. © Mahesh Joshi, Gaurav Rastogi, and J.R. Klein (2022).
DOI: 10.1093/oso/9780192847133.003.0018

dynamics, and character traits that grab the listener's attention and imagination. It helps them make sense of the focal events involved in the story. People who are more skilled as storytellers and story interpreters are more effective communicators (Boje, 1991).

Telling stories is one of the most potent means leaders have to influence, teach, and inspire. What makes storytelling so effective for learning? For starters, storytelling forges connections among people and between people and ideas. Stories convey the culture, history, and values that unite people. When it comes to countries, communities, and families, people intuitively understand that the stories they hold in common are an important part of the ties that bind. This understanding also holds true in the business world, where an organisation's stories, and the stories its leaders tell, help solidify relationships, whereas factual statements encapsulated in bullet points or numbers do not (Monarth, 2014).

Good stories do more than create a sense of connection. They build familiarity and trust and allow the listener to enter the story where they are, making them more open to learning. Good stories can contain multiple meanings, so they are surprisingly economical in conveying complex ideas in graspable ways. And stories are more engaging than a dry recitation of data points or a discussion of abstract ideas. Take the example of a company meeting. At Company A, the leader presents the financial results for the quarter. At Company B, the leader tells a rich story about what went into the 'win' that put the quarter over the top. Company A employees come away from the meeting knowing they made their numbers. Company B employees learned about an effective strategy in which sales, marketing, and product development came together to secure a significant deal. Employees now have new knowledge and new thinking to draw on. They have been influenced. They have learned (Monarth, 2014).

Another storytelling aspect that makes it so effective is that it works for all learners. In any group, roughly 40% will be predominantly visual learners who learn best from videos, diagrams, or illustrations. Another 40% will be auditory, learning best through lectures and discussions. The remaining 20% are kinaesthetic learners, who learn best by doing, experiencing, or feeling. Storytelling has aspects that work for all three types. Visual learners appreciate the mental pictures storytelling evokes. Auditory learners focus on the words and the storyteller's voice. Kinaesthetic learners remember the emotional connections and feelings from the story (Monarth, 2014).

Storytelling also helps with learning because stories are easy to remember. Organisational psychologist Peg Neuhauser found that learning that stems from a well-told story is remembered more accurately and for far longer than learning derived from facts and figures. Similarly, psychologist Jerome Bruner's research suggests that facts are 20 times more likely to be remembered if they're part of a story. Kendall Haven, the author of *Story Proof* and *Story Smart* (Haven, 2007, 2014), considers storytelling a serious business for business. He writes: 'Your goal in every communication is to influence your target audience (change their current attitudes, belief, knowledge, and behaviour). Information alone rarely changes any of these. Research confirms that well-designed stories are the most effective vehicles for exerting influence.' Stories about professional mistakes and what leaders learned from them are another great avenue for learning. Because people identify so closely with stories, imagining how they would have acted in similar circumstances, they can work through situations in a risk-free way. The extra benefit for leaders with a simple personal story is that they have conveyed underlying values, offered insight into the evolution of their own experience and knowledge, presented themselves as more approachable, and most likely inspired others to want to know more (Monarth, 2014).

## It Is About the Brain

Storytelling excels over other forms of organisational communication for a reason, and this can be explained by taking a deeper look into the human brain and how it functions. There are four main ways in which storytelling as a communication style makes a more profound impact on the listener compared to common communication strategies which involve dispensing information and data.

First, storytelling activates a function in the brain called 'neural coupling', which enables the listener to convert the ideas presented in the story into their ideas and experiences. This makes the content in the communication strategy more personal and relatable.

Second, storytelling creates a mirroring pattern in the brain, which allows the listeners to experience similar brain activity with each other and the storyteller. This enables team understanding and builds motivation amongst the listeners.

Third, when a person listens to an emotionally charged piece of communication, as happens in the case of a story, the brain releases a chemical called dopamine which stimulates memory and helps the person remember that piece of communication accurately and for a more extended period.

Finally, Paul J. Zak, a professor at Claremont Graduate University and President of Ofactor, Inc., talks about a neurochemical called oxytocin, which is released when people feel safe or are shown kindness, and it motivates cooperation with others. In his experiments, Zak found that this chemical is synthesised during character-driven stories and narratives, which generates emotions like empathy and collaboration, creating reliability and willingness to work with others. This can be especially useful when creating communication strategies for change communication or sharing difficult news with employees (Nandy, 2017).

Thanks to neural coupling, a story activates parts of the brain that allow the listener to tune into their ideas and experience. Listeners will experience similar brain activity to each other and the speaker. The brain releases dopamine into the system when it experiences an emotionally charged event, making it easier to remember and with greater accuracy. When processing facts, two brain areas are activated (Broca and Wernicke areas). A well-told story can engage many additional areas, including the motor cortex, sensory cortex, and frontal cortex (Nandy, 2017).

In an organisation, a person is bombarded with information throughout the day. This information comes to them in presentations, discussions, reports, memos, emails, and conversations. When the brain receives information in the form of stories instead of data and numbers, the inclination to capture, recollect, and reproduce that information is higher. Thus when people need to be motivated, or action is desired out of them, communication in the form of stories will generate a more robust reaction when compared to passive data (Nandy, 2017).

## But This Is Business

There has been a tangential shift in the way communication is being approached in organisations today. Storytelling can be used in various ways to improve communication in organisations. This is a tangential shift from a formal directive method of communication to a more engaging and inclusive conversational style. The distance between the sender and the receiver is getting shorter, and the need for inclusivity and relationship building through communication is getting stronger. One of the major reasons for this shift is the evolution of the workforce and the relationships they hope to make in the workplace. Formality and hierarchy have made way for equality and a flatter organisation structure (Nandy, 2017).

The image of an organisation has evolved from being a mere machine to a sociocultural system. This change in the image and characteristics of an organisation has also led to a change in the way communication strategies are created and deployed. The focus of organisations has shifted from systems to people (Nandy, 2017).

Today, employees are the most important asset of an organisation, and communication systems are like the body's nervous system, connecting the people and the work. In a practical sense, communication cannot be defined by a simple model involving a sender, a receiver, and a message. This system consists of the sender's and receiver's emotions and feelings and the way they interpret and act on the message. In this very subjective art of interpretation and conviction to action, storytelling excels over any other means of organisational communication (Nandy, 2017).

Stories can be heard everywhere in an organisation. Stories are being shared in the cafeteria line, just outside the boardroom, in the boardroom, at the water cooler, in the elevator, and just about anywhere else one cares to stop and listen. People have been telling stories ever since anyone can remember; then why has so much attention been given to stories in organisations over the last few decades? And more importantly, as human resources professionals, why should we give this new wave of communication our due attention (Nandy, 2017)?

Storytelling can be described as the art of communication using stories and narratives. This practice has derived from the age-old tradition of folklore and cultural stories passed down generation after generation verbally and often in the written form. Commonly they are called grandmother stories—narratives of identity, history, individuality, and culture (Nandy, 2017).

The value of storytelling is also far more pragmatic than history, legacy, or science may suggest. Any salesperson, marketing associate, or human relations director will testify to the value of a good story. When it comes to ideas in business, there is most likely a story behind them. Stories provide the context, so customers, stakeholders, and shareholders understand the value of the offered service, product, or solution. Using storytelling in this way helps the audience connect with the teller and establish a foundation for trusting the teller, and therefore they trust the brand. This is especially the case when the story is relatable, which also has the added benefit of being easier to understand and more memorable as it is personally relevant. The audience can see themselves as the character in the story.

Consumers are exposed to so much information, so it is easy for a business to be lost in the noise. A business may be selling something that is better than its competitors. Still, decision-making is more emotional than logical, so telling a story can help distinguish your company from competitors. Storytelling can form a powerful marketing strategy. People want to connect with brands and businesses, and the best advertisements do this by being relatable or evoking emotions. A good brand campaign should also be transparent: for example, telling people what the business struggle was and how it pulled through. This will lead the audience to care about the teller and the product or service.

The story must be consistent across all mediums, e.g. adverts, social media, the company's website, and employees. The goal is to have the audience understand the vision, and a consistent brand story will do this (Thompson, 2018).

Employees are the heart of the business. They are the company's best asset, and a business only succeeds when its employees do. However, research indicates widespread non-engagement. For example, Gallup's research suggests that 70% of U.S. employees are not engaged or are actively disengaged from work. Cultivating the right culture can be done by using storytelling. This goes beyond sharing a successful vision. Instead, share stories about the company's history, struggles, values, aims, and legacy. Share what's important with employees. Explaining what this means for them gives them something to believe in, and consequently that belief will motivate them and increase performance. This is essentially giving employees a greater sense of purpose and meaning by making them part of the company's wider story (Thompson, 2018).

The most successful companies have deep and thoughtful stories that stir a sense of larger purpose and meaning into what they do, such as Google and Apple, which are not just businesses but brands made by visionaries who want to transform the world. Consumers want to buy from companies that they believe care about something other than profits. This has been highlighted in the 2015 Lady Geek Global Empathy Index (Parmar, 2016). Businesses near the top of the list were amongst the most profitable and fastest-growing companies globally. The top ten companies also generated 50% more income than and increased in value more than twice that of companies in the bottom ten. The former use storytelling to show their company's empathetic nature, which has contributed to their success (Parmar, 2016).

The best stories evoke emotional reactions. People genuinely relate to and connect with these stories, and they believe in the company and what it stands for. When people listen to a story, they feel what the protagonist of the story is feeling, so a good way of using a story to connect with an audience is to tell a story about a mistake the company made, a failure, or maybe how life was not going well in the past.

People will relate to this as most have experienced mistakes and failures. The more the audience relates or understands, the more likely they will like the company. Humans typically make emotional, not rational decisions, so evoking emotions through storytelling is a powerful tool (Thompson, 2018).

## Storytelling Misused

One of the foundational elements of storytelling is truth. It seems paradoxical to broach the subject of purposeful propagation of falsehoods. Yet, it has become a common narrative in this Age of Distraction. Rampant untruths and public scepticism plague the world. The implications these have on every aspect of business and communications are monumental. A single negative tweet or post (short story), which may or may not contain falsehoods, has the potential to cause long-standing damage to a company. As a result, it is more important now to provide compelling, authentic, and transparent communications. Powerful, truthful storytelling combined with frictionless experiences is imperative to positively influence the awareness, affinity, and action of the people who matter most to businesses (Scales, 2018).

False stories or fake news have been around as long as human civilisation, but digital technology has been turbocharged and has transformed the global media landscape. Nevertheless, defenders of fact and truth still have weapons to help uphold integrity in the social, political, and economic environments. The misinformation effect refers to the tendency for post-event information to interfere with the memory of the actual event. Researchers have shown that the introduction of even relatively subtle information following an event can dramatically affect how people remember. The misinformation effect illustrates how easily memories can be influenced. It also raises concerns about the reliability of memory, particularly when eyewitness testimony is used to determine criminal guilt. False stories that produce the misinformation effect can profoundly impact our memories. One way to counteract this is to write down the story or memory of an event immediately after it happens, which might help minimise such effects (Scales, 2018). The solution is not apparent, and the debate is energetic. The best place to start for leaders of this age is at home—in the culture built locally, where personal, organisational, and societal introspect should tell the true story.

Storytelling is the unchanging component in an environment with ever-changing components. In a disruptive and distractive ocean of information, the moment's challenge is to figure out how to emotionally bond with the person or organisations and build or design services or products that solve their problems. For business, it involves creating an organisational culture sensitive to teamwork, customer focus, fair treatment of employees, initiative, and innovation. Culture becomes the glue that holds people together. Stories represent more than the corporate culture; they help mould society's culture.

## Bibliography

Aaker, Jennifer and Andy Smith. 2010. The Dragon Fly Effect: Quick, Effective, and Powerful Ways to Use Social Media to Drive Social Change. San Francisco: Jossey-Bass

Anderson, Chris. 2017. Storytelling Is a Powerful Communication Tool. TED, 11 November. https://ideas.ted.com/storytelling-is-a-powerful-communication-tool-heres-how-to-use-it-from-ted/

Boje, D.M. 1991. Learning Storytelling: Storytelling to Learn Management Skills. *Journal of Management Education*, vol. 15, no. 3:279–294

Haven, Kendall. 2007. Story Proof: The Science Behind the Startling Power of Story. Westport, CT: Libraries Unlimited

Haven, Kendall. 2014. Story Smart: Using the Science of Story to Persuade, Influence, Inspire, and Teach. Santa Barbara: Libraries Unlimited

Li, Meng. 2020. How to Use Storytelling as Management Tool. Ohio State University, Fisher College of Business, 1 July. https://fisher.osu.edu/blogs/leadreadtoday/how-use-storytelling-management-tool

Monarth, Harrison. 2014. The Irresistible Power of Storytelling as a Strategic Business Tool. Harvard Business Review, 11 March. https://hbr.org/2014/03/the-irresistible-power-of-storytelling-as-a-strategic-business-tool

Nandy, Purnima. 2017. How Top Companies Use Storytelling to Drive Results. Insider HR, 23 March. https://www.insidehr.com.au/how-top-companies-use-storytelling-to-drive-results/

Parmar, Belinda. 2016. The Most Empathetic Companies, 2016. Harvard Business Review, 20 December. https://hbr.org/2016/12/the-most-and-least-empathetic-companies-2016

Scales, Don. 2018. Storytelling in the Age of Fake News. Forbes, 6 December. https://www.forbes.com/sites/forbesagencycouncil/2018/12/06/storytelling-in-the-age-of-fake-news/?sh=7506ad8731f9

Thompson, Sophie. 2018. The Importance of Storytelling in Business, with Examples. VirtualSpeech, 7 December. https://virtualspeech.com/blog/importance-storytelling-business

# 19

# Reinventing by Looking Forward

In the future, staying employed will be about reinventing self. It will be the single most important strategy. It is like the ouroboros, an ancient symbol depicting a serpent or dragon eating its tail, often interpreted as a symbol for eternal cyclic renewal (Oxford, 2021). This ancient symbol is strangely applicable in the Age of Distraction and Disruption. One can only speculate about the future disruptive influence of technology coupled with an unforeseen and unsettling pandemic forced upon businesses, workers, governments, and everything else. Amid that complexity, industries are already in the process of remaking themselves. Any business not actively adopting or adapting to technology is going out of business. Technical obsolescence has become a fact in the quick-paced world of technology. For example, the first iPhone launched in 2007 was a broad-brushed game changer but has joined the ranks of vinyl records because the design was based on a point in the cyclic renewal of technology. Its low-memory minimum chip speed makes it unable to handle the new software. At some point, all hardware will be obsolete. Technical obsolescence of hardware is obvious, and it is also present in the workforce. It can be seen in the 'hyphen-tech' evolution of finance, human resources, health, sales, marketing, and everything that is transforming the primary functions of business operations. Every job has an expiration date; therefore, individual workers will have to deal with the challenge of staying relevant, which will mean reinventing themselves for the next round or next iteration of the job market.

The speed of innovation in business used to be slow but has now accelerated and the introduction of new products increasing dramatically. As a company acquires technology, it begins a process of technology ingestion where the technology starts digesting the business. Technology is accelerating very sharply. In an older industry, the pace of change might be 30 or 50 years, and some jobs have not changed in 100 years. Technology is on a faster-moving treadmill, with the inevitable reinvention of jobs and careers

*Global Business in the Age of Destruction and Distraction.* Mahesh Joshi, Gaurav Rastogi, and J.R. Klein,
Oxford University Press. 
DOI: 10.1093/oso/9780192847133.003.0019

becoming extremely important. What may have earlier taken 30 years for jobs to transform now takes 5 years or less.

An example is the executive assistant. There was a strong demand for executive assistants in the workforce at one time. The position filled a logistical role of scheduling, managing an executive, arranging travel, and other logistical tasks. Innovations have reduced the number of people employed as executive assistants by 40% (Feintzeig, 2020). With technology, executives now can manage calendaring, email, contacts, travel, and most of the other logistical tasks once handled by an assistant.

Everyone and every industry are feeling the heat from the transformations. Obsolescence comes from every angle and without notice. It might be subtle things like a company recognising excess management capacity or an employee realising their job is being done by many other people or doing other people's work. It might be that workers' ideas once considered valuable are now regarded as old-fashioned and slowing down the company's change. These signals impact performance and cause frustration that might signify being obsolete. Silicon Valley workers who have been working for decades find that the generation of new employees is quite different from them—not just in terms of being younger but in their attitude towards technology, and, as a result, they work differently. These changes are complex, even for techies themselves. It is hard to keep pace with changes and it requires conscious reinvention. The key to the new game is to ride ahead of technical obsolescence. It involves awareness of the signs and signals of subtle changes and being flexible and aggressive in becoming the next relevant need in the market.

## Stuck in Former Glory

One of the problems in this ouroboros challenge is getting stuck in former glory. People tend to mark career highs as a reference for current work and future work. Though there is some value in experience and accomplishment, it can become a detriment just as quickly. The trick is not to be a 'used to be'. It becomes a matter of thinking about the value of defining oneself in a market that may no longer find former skills and attainments as applicable. Not thinking through this cognitive reinvention and holding on for too long leads to fear that career highs are now barriers to doing new things. Previous success can get in the way of future success. New thinking requires fluidity. It requires experimenting with careers, learning new things, and reinventing in a new way. This fluidity changes individual values and leads to self-realisation that changes the language of internal and external dialogue. It changes how people introduce themselves, how they approach the normal career ups and downs, and ultimately how they succeed. The game is constantly evolving.

Success can be a source of fragility. If thinking and action are too wedded to an idea or one single idea of success, it leads to not doing anything else, which creates a state of fragility. True success requires just the opposite. Nassim Taleb calls it antifragile (Taleb, 2012): when variations are introduced into an environment, they are met with a measured learned approach, reinvented thinking. The way this antifragility is developed is like any muscle is strengthened. It requires a trip to a failure gym. This involves taking the risk of failure and willingly experiencing it; again and again, the skills of dealing with failure are learned. The conquering of fear of failure is the primary strategy of success. This is the attitude needed by leaders, workers, and anyone desiring success in life.

Steve Jobs, often touted as an example of outstanding leadership, was a young man who started Apple, which launched the personal computing revolution. He went public with the company at age 25, and within a few years of being highly successful in becoming a multimillionaire, he was fired from his company at age 30. It would not be surprising for him to spend the rest of his life being a rich used to be. But within a year, he was making the moves that would ultimately bring him back into Apple. He invested in the next generation of computers, a handheld device and Pixar. Ten years later, both of these investments helped him come back to Apple when change created an environment where he was needed once again. This is an example of personal reinvention. Some segments of the workforce have already adapted. The definition of an entrepreneur is the willingness to take risks, experiment, and be successful while risking a lot more. This is an entrepreneurial world driven by technology and filled with people who have continued to come back to challenges and identifying new solutions.

## Looking Forward

The lesson to be learned is that the old stories, the stale tales, a deep identification with career highs, and dramatic drops cause embarrassment. Embarrassment alienates and often makes recovery more difficult. It is based on a skewed perception of self and deviant thinking about the inner-self and hides the recognition of the basic human traits of imagination, innovation, and reinvention. Coming down from a high is dreadful. It pulls apart security and confidence, shattering comfort, and blinds thinking into assuming it will be permanent. But just as the highs are not permanent, neither are the lows. The only reason for their perseverance is holding on to the memory of the highs at the expense of disengagement with the present. Reinvention is simply a question of standing at one place and looking forward or back. The choice of looking back at career history or looking forward to making history requires a change in the frame of mind. It poses the question of what kind of future can be created.

Knowing successes and failures gives way to humility, building confidence, and engaging. In the 1980s, 1990s, and 2000s, there were a plethora of business books based on some company name and espousing the value of doing things that way. They were huge sellers because people thought there must be something that these companies were doing differently and should be emulated. From today's perspective, something interesting is revealed. Those strategies and ideas no longer work and have vanished, as have many companies. Many of them became so enamoured in reading their own books that they did not recognise that change was overtaking them, and it became a sure-fire recipe for disaster.

The innovation part of the human brain can be constrained by the shackles of only doing things one way and rationalising the effect of always getting the same results. This is fertile ground for automation's propensity to handle the predictability of symmetric thinking. Tesla, for example, was not an automotive company. There were many companies making automobiles, and such companies were moderately innovative. For years, they were successful at repeating the same thing with a bit more spit and polish. They created a concept monopoly where it could not be done if it was not their idea. Into their world comes a disrupter who had nothing to do with the industry, nothing to do with the technology, no experience, and no knowledge of the 'best' way to do things. Tesla is a disruptive influence on the auto industry, changing everything that has for so long been sacred. The biggest worry for most companies and individuals is the thinking that says this is the best way to do it, or we have got this nailed down. Reality reveals that somewhere in some part of the world is thinking about a better idea that can, in an instance, make any industry, any worker irrelevant.

The impact of this symmetrical thinking is universal. The retreat from thinking and confronting the concept of reinvention will affect not only the individual or business, but also everyone and everything. The lesson of interconnectivity is exemplified in accepting or ignoring this concept. Whether intended or not, its presence in the world puts us in the middle of real life. There are family, friends, workmates, teammates, social relationships, community, and cultural roles and identities, all of which are connected. Even the most reclusive individuals have an innate connection to nature or creation that is inescapable. Everyone suffers, whether it is acknowledged or not when someone suffers, because all are connected in an intrinsic technological web. This is a world where someone on the other side of the globe getting a viral infection puts everyone at risk.

## Being Reinvented

Reinvention has a lot to do with rethinking and with building new habits. Many conversations, for example, begin with a harmless phrase like 'What are you doing these days?' The response is often rehearsed, with throwbacks to former events or career highlights the answer. These responses usually carry little more than a short version of a resume and certainly have little to do with 'these days'. It is certainly not a way to invite a two-way conversation. Psychologists tell us that part of the framing of reinvention falls in the lap of the way the initial question is asked. Instead of 'What are you doing these days?' framing the question in a more interesting way might stimulate thoughtful dialogue. For example, if someone asked, 'What are you working on or building these days?' the answer initiates a different way of thinking and encourages a different kind of answer. Maybe asking about current obsessions or passion or work challenges and engaging with passionate listening and response will infuse energy into the conversation. This habit is emblematic of a reinventive mindset and provides both external and internal benefits.

Think about career and personal reinvention. It is not about looking back at your history mountain but about today's playing field and how to stay relevant in it. It involves constantly evolving and reinventing to present an interesting, engaging, knowledgeable, and flexible leader, worker, or individual. The concept of personal reinvention encourages celebrating successful benchmarks and moving on to the next thing. It is the epitome of the Yiddish saying, 'Do what is next'.

## Bibliography

Feintzeig, Rachel. 2020. The Vanishing Executive Assistant. *Wall Street Journal*, 18 January. https://www.wsj.com/articles/the-vanishing-executive-assistant-11579323605

Oxford. 2021. *Oxford English Dictionary*. Oxford: Oxford University Press

Taleb, Nassim Nicholas. 2012. *Antifragile: Things That Gain from Disorder*. New York: Random House

# 20
# Humans in the Future Workforce

The fear of technological innovation destroying jobs and displacing workers dates back several hundred years, even before the Luddite movement in Britain during the Industrial Revolution which gave its name to militant technophobia. The Luddites were textile mill workers in Nottingham who rioted in 1811 to destroy the new automated looms that threatened their livelihoods. Ever since, there has been no shortage of predictions that machines would replace human labourers, with possibly dire effects (Manyika et al., 2017). Karl Marx wrote in 1858 that 'the means of labour passes through different metamorphoses, whose culmination is the machine, or rather, an automatic system of machinery' (McLellan, 1971).

Advances in robotics, artificial intelligence, and machine learning are ushering in a new age of automation, as machines match or outperform human performance in various work activities, including ones requiring cognitive capabilities. The McKinsey report (Manyika et al., 2017) estimates that 50% of the activities that people are paid to do in the global economy have the potential to be automated by adapting currently demonstrated technology. At a global level, technically automatable activities touch the equivalent of 1.2 billion employees and $14.6 trillion in wages. Four economies, China, India, Japan, and the United States, account for over half of these total wages and employees. China and India together account for the largest technically automatable employment, potentially more than 700 million full-time equivalents between them, because of the relative size of their labour forces. The potential is also significant in Europe: according to our analysis, 62 million full-time employee equivalents and more than $1.9 trillion in wages are associated with technically automatable activities in the five largest economies (France, Germany, Italy, Spain, and the United Kingdom) (Manyika et al., 2017).

In 2013, Oxford Martin School examined the expected impacts of future computerisation on U.S. labour market outcomes. The primary objective was analysing the number of jobs at risk and the relationship between an occupation's probability of computerisation, wages, and educational

*Global Business in the Age of Destruction and Distraction.* Mahesh Joshi, Gaurav Rastogi, and J.R. Klein, Oxford University Press. 
DOI: 10.1093/oso/9780192847133.003.0020

attainment. According to their estimates, about 47% of total U.S. employment was at risk (Frey and Osborne, 2013). About 60% of occupations have at least 30% technically automatable activities. Activities with the highest automation potential were ones with predictable physical activities (81%), processing data (69%), and collecting data (64%) (Manyika et al., 2017).

The global workforce has changed dramatically, and technological transformation has spawned exponential freelancing that has overturned the nature of employment and talent management. As freelancers gain a better understanding of industries and labour markets, they have leveraged this knowledge with decisive strategies to market their talents. The result is that they earn more, are happier at work and in their private and social lives in general, and scale work and play anytime they want or need. In short, digital transformation and the rise of freelancing have disrupted employment, with talent now dictating a company's strategy and speed of innovation (Gilber, 2021). Freelancers represent around 35% of the global workforce of 3.5 billion. That means 1.1 billion workers are on a digital platform. Even before the current 2019 pandemic, freelancing was touted as one of the fastest-growing employment sectors in the world. Businesses saw large increases in freelancers in North America and other countries. Freelance job postings rose by 41% during the second quarter of 2020, partially due to the current pandemic (Schulz, 2021). The growth of freelance work is not expected to slow down, as more and more professionals see it as a viable option for both part-time and full-time work in the long run. It is estimated that global freelancers contribute around $23.16–42.9 trillion to the world economy annually (Gilber, 2021). These two trends, automation and remote work, will continue to change the future of human workers.

## The Paradox of Change

The paradox of change in the human workforce is based first on education and skill expectations for workers. It used to be that becoming a lifetime employee of a company was the thing to do. As the technological revolution demands more high-end skills, the prospect of staying at a company long enough to retire has dwindled. Workers must be exposed to newer technologies and new learning to remain relevant. Careers were of two primary types: micro-tasking and macro-tasking. The job entailed simple tasks like assembling components, delivering products, or picking apples. Macro-tasks require more calculating or mental thinking, like what product to manufacture or how to move sales into a specific market. Higher-level skills also need some understanding of human interactions.

Most companies had a corporate model where tasking was fully vertically integrated throughout the organisation. There has been a rise in another form of the corporate model called virtual cooperation. Apple and Amazon are examples of this model. They do not manufacture anything and are specifically designed to market products. Virtual companies need more macro-taskers or higher-skilled workers. Demand for these skills has become more urgent than it has ever been. Workers no longer need to be an encyclopaedia of skill and expertise that understands every detailed complexity.

The stability of micro- and macro-tasking in the business world has been a staple for a long time. The axiom of 'change, changes, changing' has become prevalent, with virtual corporations, automation, and online opportunities spilling through the front door. These changes drive how people work and how the work environment continues to change in the future. This phenomenon raises a conversation about the dominant–submissive dynamic of the human and technology culture. Just as fire has impacted humans' ability to feed their brains by allowing for the 'predigestion' of food, facilitating glucose delivery to the brain, and language has enabled coordinated efforts between people, today's technology will reshape human beings. As money, railways, electricity, and now artificial intelligence again inform the co-evolution of man and machine, the same philosophical question arises. Will humans be the masters of technology or its slaves? The speed of change is creating massive societal changes, and everyone will have to adjust quickly until the relationship stabilises. The luxury afforded by previous change with its timeline of lifetimes, generations, decades, or years to adjust is no longer available. Changes in technology become a wicked mistress demanding dominance.

It is convenient to believe that people are the masters of technology and have complete freedom of movement and action. A counter-argument looks at the algorithms and technologies that dictate what to read, eat, and wear, and how to act. For example, workers involved in micro-tasks are assigned as pieces of work. An Uber driver is told where to go, who to pick up, where to drop them, and then what to do next. Work is being assigned by technology, and the question is which is dominant and which is submissive. The dynamic between automation, artificial intelligence, robots, or software, on the one hand, is distracting, and, on the other hand, it is taking away jobs that require low attention spans. The central issue is the creative ability to use technology for human benefit and not be used by it.

How does humanity retain dominance? Part of it is to wake up and smell the roses. The cycle of learn and work has changed a lot. Expecting to simply work, then retirement is no longer applicable. The old model of study, work, and retirement has become learn, work, relearn, work, and enjoy. In 2020, 42% of core skills required to perform existing jobs were expected to change by 2022. In addition to high-tech skills, specialised interpersonal skills will be in high demand, including sales, human resources, care, and education (Zahidi, 2020).

The world is facing a reskilling emergency. On the personal side, mastery in a field like radiology that demanded specific art and skills is now performed by software that can read an X-ray more accurately than a seasoned radiologist and in a fraction of the time. The coveted ability to be an expert in typing has given way to voice recognition that can type many times faster and with marked excellence that outpaces any human. The organisational conundrum is sorting out the role of people and machines. The impact on society with regard to education, skill development, wages, integration, work standards, economic factors, inequality, and unemployment will all come into play. The machine dominance in these scenarios can be complex and alarming.

The big challenge for humanity may be summed up in the opening words of English journalist Rudyard Kipling's poem *If*:

> If you can keep your head when all about you
> Are losing theirs and blaming it on you,
> If you can trust yourself when all men doubt you,
> But make allowance for their doubting too;
> If you can wait and not be tired by waiting,
> Or being lied about, don't deal in lies,
> Or being hated, don't give way to hating,
> And yet don't look too good, nor talk too wise:

The challenge of humanity is to remember we are human. The human legacy of innovation, initiative, and interaction must be resurrected again. There are no rules or understanding about how businesses, companies, countries, or politics operate that are not changing. There are no benchmarks to compare, no rules of thumb, no sticky notes to refresh memory. Whether leaders, workers, or just plain folk, people must learn to live in the present. They have to learn to engage reality on its own terms with no reference to rules that are most likely no longer useful.

## Engaging Reality

To conquer the concept of engaging reality, the first thing to ponder is learning itself. Humans distinguish themselves from other animals by their possession of cognitive facilities; they are capable of critical thinking and the ability to make thought-based decisions. Learning is the fairy power, the *raison d'être*, the magic key that will provide superhuman reliance and ongoing relevance in today's workplace. Today's learning is more learning by doing than learning by reading. It is about translating knowledge into measurable action and understanding the value of experience beyond knowing. It is hands-on messing around with the technology and learning to understand by making mistakes and building intuition. It is learning that may not be fluent in that particular aspect but which builds upon what did not work to find a better way. The storyline is no longer linear and is open to the environment's changes and learning how to flow with it.

The next piece of engagement is mastery. This begins with knowing and disciplining oneself in the spiritual, emotional, mental, and physical realms of existence. It involves mastering the art of telling one's own story and the art of changing it as times and the environment change. It is also learning how to use learning. Much learning is in the head from education or reading and is initially sufficient for success. As the nature of the world has changed and become much more hands-on, the challenge is mastering the ability not to let the head get in the way, allowing intuition, innovation, and sometimes passion and emotion to take sway. Some would say that controlled discipline is the key to success for human workers in a fast-changing environment.

The next level of engaging reality is connections or the mastery of relationships. This involves learning empathy. It goes beyond simply what is expected to an understanding of the concept of caring for people and being able to frame things in a way that helps other people understand the story. It involves learning and understanding how to influence people with a far more comprehensive range of capabilities than simply writing something up and expecting people to follow through. It is the ability to engage people, to move and excite them with the story or the cause.

And finally, engaging reality is learning how to pivot. It is the capacity to lean into the change, knowing when and how to resist change, when to adapt, and when to embrace it. It is the ability to tell a new story every time something changes and take advantage of the changing events. The ability to pivot will be essential.

## Humans Are Humans

During the Industrial Revolution it paid to have people work and think like machines—like machinery, they were expected to show up at the workplace at a specific time, work for 8 or 12 hours, and then return home. Workers were essentially a cog in the wheel of a large industrial machine. The effect on workers that do such work, who are plugged in all the time, with no ability to unplug, is low levels of engagement and performance. Productivity is not directly correlated to hours worked. Today, the generally accepted axiom is that humans are not machines, but machines are becoming more human, including their cognitive capability. The need is not for humans to be more machine-like; it is for humans to be more human. In the future, anything that can be automated will be automated, and not only micro-tasks but also some macro-tasks.

To be dominant in a technologically distracting world begins with the personal decisions that feed all of society's institutions. It involves learning how to recognise and control distractions. It requires building physical, emotional, mental, and spiritual capacity. This 'spiritual' grounding is core to operating in the modern workplace. It enables finding personal sources of motivation, determination and endurance, internal energy, and purpose. These competencies feed the world that surrounds everyone. It will clear thinking, clarify passion, and drive action. This path will facilitate renewal, reinvention, and restoration, which are part and parcel of an evolving cultural and social system. It will be the framework for co-evolving with technology and setting the standards of being served by rather than serving it.

## Bibliography

Frey, Carl Benedikt and Michael Osborne. 2013. The Future of Employment: How Susceptible Are Jobs to Computerisation? Oxford: Oxford Martin School, p.38

Gilber, Nestor. 2021. 405 Freelance Statistics for 2021: Market Size, Profile Data & Salary Rates. Finances Online, 2 August. https://financesonline.com/freelance-statistics/

Manyika, James, Michael Chui, Mehdi Miremadi, et al. 2017. A Future That Works: Automation, Employment, and Productivity. New York: McKinsey Global Institute, McKinsey and Company

McLellan, David (ed.) 1971. The Grundrisse. New York: Harper & Row

Schulz, Stefan. 2021. 54 Freelance Statistics, Trends, and Insights. DDIY (Don't Do It Yourself), 2 August. https://ddiy.co/freelance-statistics/

Zahidi, Saadia. 2020. We Need a Global Reskilling Revolution—Here's Why. World Economic Forum, 22 January. https://www.weforum.org/agenda/2020/01/reskilling-revolution-jobs-future-skills/

# Index